THE PRAGMATICS OF LEFT DETACHMENT
IN SPOKEN STANDARD FRENCH

Pragmatics & Beyond

An Interdisciplinary Series of Language Studies

Editors:

Herman Parret
*(Belgian National Science Foundation,
Universities of Louvain and Antwerp)*

Jef Verschueren
*(Belgian National Science Foundation,
University of Antwerp)*

Editorial Address:

Department of Germanic Languages and Literatures
University of Antwerp (UIA)
Universiteitsplein 1
B-2610 Wilrijk
Belgium

Editorial Board:

Norbert Dittmar *(Free University of Berlin)*
David Holdcroft *(University of Leeds)*
Jacob Mey *(Odense University)*
Jerrold M. Sadock *(University of Chicago)*
Emanuel A. Schegloff *(University of California at Los Angeles)*
Daniel Vanderveken *(University of Quebec at Trois-Rivières)*
Teun A. van Dijk *(University of Amsterdam)*

VI:3

Betsy K. Barnes

The Pragmatics of Left Detachment in Spoken Standard French

THE PRAGMATICS OF LEFT DETACHMENT
IN SPOKEN STANDARD FRENCH

Betsy K. Barnes
University of Minnesota

JOHN BENJAMINS PUBLISHING COMPANY
AMSTERDAM/PHILADELPHIA

1985

Library of Congress Cataloging in Publication Data

Barnes, Betsy K.
  The pragmatics of left detachment in spoken standard French.

  (Pragmatics & beyond, ISSN 0166-6258; VI:3)
Bibliography: p.
1. French language -- Syntax. 2. French language -- Spoken French. I. Title. II. Series.
PC2361.B37   1985   445   85-26773
ISBN 90 272 2545 1 (European) / ISBN 0-915027-65-8 (US) (alk. paper)

© Copyright 1985 - John Benjamins B.V.
No part of this book may be reproduced in any form, by print, photoprint, microfilm, or any other means, without written permission from the publisher.

TABLE OF CONTENTS

ACKNOWLEDGMENTS	vii
1. INTRODUCTION	1
1.1. Purposes of the study	1
1.2. The language of the corpus	2
2. REVIEW OF THE LITERATURE	5
2.1. Syntactic descriptions and the syntactic-pragmatic correlation hypothesis (SPCH)	5
2.2. Pragmatic descriptions	9
3. THE DATA–GENERAL OBSERVATIONS AND HYPOTHESES	13
3.1. Preliminary observations	13
3.2. Problems with the syntactic-pragmatic correlation hypothesis	16
3.2.1. LD in contrastive contexts	16
3.2.2. Introduction of new referents	19
3.3. Contrastiveness and topic shift	21
3.4. A new hypothesis — in search of LDs of minimal pragmatic motivation	24
3.5. Alternative syntactic analyses	26
3.6. The 'domain' of LD: sentence-topic and discourse-topic	28
3.6.1. The notion of discourse-topic	28
3.6.2. LD, sentence-topic, and discourse-topic in the corpus	31
4. PRONOMINAL DETACHMENTS	37
4.1. 'Personal' pronouns: first person: *moi, nous*	37
4.2. 'Nonpersonal' pronoun: *ça*	45
5. LEXICAL NP DETACHMENTS	49
5.1. With nonpersonal anaphor	49
5.1.1. NP *c'est* ...	49
5.1.2. NP *ça* V	58

5.2.	With personal anaphor: NP *il/elle* ...	59
	5.2.1. LD and information statuses — background	60
	5.2.2. The data	62
	(I) Introduction and summary	62
	(II) LD with Evoked referents	63
	(III) LD with New referents	68
	5.2.3. LD and the *ya*-cleft	75
	5.2.4. LD vs. NP-subjects: the grounding principle	80
5.3.	NP-LDs with nonsubject anaphors	89
5.4.	The definiteness constraint	92
6. SPECIAL CASES	95
6.1.	'Topicalization' and 'Focus Movement' in spoken French	95
6.2.	No-anaphor LDs	98
6.3.	Double LDs	104
7. CONCLUSION	111
NOTES	115
REFERENCES	121

ACKNOWLEDGMENTS

I am especially grateful fo Knud Lambrecht for his careful reading of much of this work and the many helpful suggestions he provided. My thanks also to George Yule for some comments and encouragement.

This research was supported by a grant from the Graduate School of the University of Minnesota.

1. INTRODUCTION

1.1. Purposes of the study

To describe the present object of study with maximal generality (and neutrality), I prefer to borrow Kayne's (1975) term, 'left detachment' constructions. This term refers to any of a number of constructions occurring in French and other languages characterized by the occurrence, to the immediate left of an already syntactically complete sentence, of an NP, PP or pronoun, which is ordinarily 'doubled', so to speak, by a coreferential pronoun within the sentence. The following illustrate some of the possibilities:

(1)   a.   Moi je bois énormément.
       b.   Ta soupe, elle arrive rose.
       c.   Ma soeur, on lui a coupé les cheveux.
(2)   A ma soeur, on lui a coupé les cheveux.

A related construction often grouped with these is that referred to as Topicalization, where a left-detached element has no coreferential pronoun in the accompanying clause, e.g.:

(3)   a.   Les haricots j'aime bien.
       b.   A Pierre je parle tout le temps.

It should also be noted that, while the lefthand element is detached in the sense that it is in no way syntactically integrated into the accompanying sentence, it is not necessarily set off phonologically from the sentence. That is, there is no necessary pause, and the detachment may or may not have its own intonation contour. (Prosodic features of the various constructions will be discussed in more detail below.)

Such constructions have been studied in considerable detail with respect to their syntactic properties and possible formal analyses within the generative-transformational framework (Cinque 1977; Larsson 1979). In addition, some linguists (Larsson 1979; Galambos 1980; Lambrecht 1981) have addressed the question of the pragmatic function of these constructions. However, even in these studies, despite some very insightful and important observations, particularly in Lambrecht (1981) and his more recent work, the pragmatic descriptions remain quite general, and they are not usually based primarily on examination of an actual corpus of oral discourse. It is for this reason that I have undertaken to examine the occurrence of these constructions in a corpus of spontaneous language. The general purposes of the study are the following:

(a) Syntactic comparison of left detachment constructions found in the corpus with those described in the literature, i.e. syntactic description of detachment constructions in a particular variety of French, namely informal spoken Standard French.[1]

(b) Formulation of more precise descriptions of the pragmatic function(s) of each type of detachment construction occurring in the corpus, through examination of contexts in which each occurs.

1.2. The language of the corpus

Grammarians and linguists have long observed the fact that at least some of the constructions shown above ((1)a-c, i.e. those with detached NP or Pro) are extremely frequent in nonstandard varieties of French usually referred to as *français populaire*.[2] Galambos (1981) even goes so far as to claim that 'popular spoken French', as exemplified in Queneau's *Zazie dans le métro*, is a topic-prominent language, in the sense of Li and Thompson (1976), on the basis of the prevalence in this variety of French of structures like those of (1) above. Given the apparent ubiquitousness of these constructions in the nonstandard dialects, the choice of a corpus representing what may be called colloquial standard French presents certain advantages. First, it should throw some light on the question of just how frequent the various types of these constructions are in this variety of French (information which carries interesting implications for the pedagogy of French). Secondly, the very fact that such constructions are apparently less frequent in this variety might facilitate the determination of those pragmatic factors which constrain or favor their occurrence.

With regard to the preceding remarks concerning the association of certain detachment constructions with popular or nonstandard French, I should note that this is an inexact characterization of the descriptions of some observers. In fact, even some of the earliest discussions of these structures are noteworthy for the fact that the structures are associated not simply with the popular language, but with the spoken language in general. Bally (1932: 70), for example, relates the greater frequency of such constructions in the spoken as opposed to the written language, to the particular conditions on perceptual processing which characterize oral communication. Similarly, Bauche (1928: 155-56) observes that "pour la construction générale [de la phrase], il n'y a pas de véritable différence entre le langage populaire et le français *parlé* [Bauche's underlining]. Il en est autrement avec le francais écrit." Bauche goes on to argue that the prevalence of the relevant detachment constructions in the spoken language is motivated by what one could summarize as the need for greater expressivity which characterizes the spoken language. He then concludes with the following: "Or c'est du langage parlé, c'est donc, à un certain point de vue, populaire, puisque le peuple emploie la langue parlée et non la langue écrite. Mais c'est aussi du français correct, en tant que français parlé" (156). While analyses such as Bally's and Bauche's may be lacking somewhat in precision, I believe they do point to certain aspects of the function of these constructions which have been largely neglected in recent work on their use in French, namely the fact the the use of at least some of them should be related to the unplanned nature of oral discourse.[3]

It might be useful at this point to give a rough description of the kind of language found in the corpus being used here. To do this, I would like to make use of the list of features given by Lambrecht (1981: 6-7) as "grammatical features of Non-Standard French relevant in the context of [his] paper." It should be noted that Lambrecht uses the term Non-Standard French for approximately the same variety of French as is being studied here, i.e. colloquial standard French, or simply spoken French. Informal observation of the present corpus yields the following observations (using Lambrecht's descriptions and examples of the features):[4]

(a) Features which occur consistently
  (i) Replacement of *nous* VERB-*ons* by *on* VERB
  (ii) Complex shifts in the pronoun system:
    in particular:
    cela → *ça   cela me plaît* → *ça me plaît*
    use of clitic *ça* for generic referents: *la mer ça me plaît*
  (iii) Final elimination of (suffixally inflected) simple past and replacement by present perfect:
    il arriva → *il est arrivé*
  (iv) Greater use of 'analytic' tenses, in particular for the future:
    il viendra → *il va venir, il veut venir*
  (v) Elimination of clitic-verb inversion [in yes-no questions] and

optional character of question movement:
où vas-tu? → où tu vas? → tu vas où?

(b) Features which alternate with corresponding standard features, where both realizations are relatively frequent
  (i) Elimination of the negative clitic *ne*:
  il ne vient pas → il vient pas
  (ii) Increased phonetic erosion of clitic pronouns:
  tu as → t-as, il me voit → i-m-voit
  (iii) Loss of 'grammatical subjects':
  il faut → faut, il y a → y a

(c) Features which alternate with corresponding standard features, where the nonstandard feature is of relatively low frequency
  (i) Replacement of relative pronoun *qui* by *que*:
  l'homme qui fait ça → l'homme que fait ça
  (ii) Loss of analytic case marking in the relative pronoun:
  l'homme de qui je cause → l'homme que je cause

As to lexical features, the corpus is for the most part quite 'correct', except for the very occasional occurrence of a nonstandard term, most often of the type traditionally referred to as *familier*, e.g. *bouffer, draguer, môme*.

While it is clear that the style of this language sample is relatively casual, these same speakers would no doubt use a yet more casual style in other more natural situations, e.g. at home or with intimates or peers only.[5] Yet there is evidence that much of this sample may be described, in Labov's terms (1972: 86), as spontaneous speech, i.e. "a pattern used in excited, emotionally charged speech when the constraints of a formal situation are overridden". Evidence for this claim is furnished by the 'channel cues' of relative tempo, pitch, and volume (95).

2. REVIEW OF THE LITERATURE

A brief sketch will be given of the development of the syntactic analyses, in particular as these relate to pragmatic descriptions. A very complete summary of these developments can be found in Larsson (1979). There has been relatively little discussion of the structures in (3) above with respect to French. I will delay any discussion of these 'topicalized' structures until sec. 6.1 below.

2.1. Syntactic descriptions and the syntactic-pragmatic correlation hypothesis (SPCH)

This section will include some consideration of pragmatic functions, since one of my particular purposes is the empirical testing of a correlation between syntactic origin and pragmatic function which is suggested in some of the syntactic descriptions.

In his 1967 thesis, Ross suggested that structures such as those in (1) (in English) be derived by a transformational copying rule of Left Dislocation:

(4) Left Dislocation (Ross 1967: 233-34)
 X - NP - Y ⇒ 2#[1 [2]3]
 1   2   3   +PRO

That is, example (1b) above would be derived from (5a), and both (1c) and (2) from (5b):

(5) a. Ta soupe arrive rose.
 b. On a coupé les cheveux à ma soeur.

Hirschbühler (1975) points out the existence of certain types of left detachment constructions which cannot be derived by the rule of Left Dislocation due to the peculiar nature of the relation between the lefthand element and the anaphoric expression in the clause. The following are representative:

(6) a. Paul, Pierre vient de se battre avec cet idiot.
 b. La grande blonde qui est là-bas, je pense que j'ai déjà vu cette tête-là quelque part.
 c. Un espion, on le reconnaît à son chapeau.
 d. Un espion, on reconnaît cela à son chapeau.

To handle these cases, Hirschbühler proposes, as an alternative to the LD analysis, an extension of the base rules to allow structures with lefthand NPs to be generated as deep structures, provided that the lefthand NP is anaphorically related to an NP (or PP) in the accompanying clause. At the same time, Hirschbühler notes that the LD analysis appears to be the correct analysis for constructions with a lefthand PP, since these constructions, unlike those with a lefthand NP, are subject to Ross's constraints on movement rules.[6]

Cinque (1977) takes up and elaborates on Hirschbühler (1975), using evidence primarily from Italian and French to argue that we in fact have to do with two different constructions, the ones with lefthand PPs being transformationally derived by the LD rule, and those with lefthand NPs where a transformational origin is excluded (e.g. (6) above) being base-generated. The principal distinctive syntactic features enumerated by Cinque can be summarized by the following lists of features which are claimed to be grammatical only in the given construction type, and which can thus be taken as proof of a particular origin:

(a) Transformationally derived
  (i) Lefthand element is a PP (where the preposition is governed by the verb).
  (ii) The lefthand element and its anaphor occur within an embedded S.
  (iii) The lefthand element is part of an idiom.
  (iv) (In Italian) the lefthand element contains the reflexive possessive adjective *proprio*.[7]

(b) Base-generated
  (i) Anaphor of lefthand element is an NP (epithet or definite description).
  (ii) Lefthand element and its pronominal anaphor differ in some grammatical feature (e.g. definiteness), i.e. lack of agreement, as in (6c) and (6d) above.[8]
  (iii) The anaphoric expression is a nonclitic pronoun, e.g.:
  $\begin{Bmatrix} \text{*A Pierre} \\ \text{Pierre} \end{Bmatrix}$, je pense toujours à lui.
  (iv) One of Ross's island constraints is violated, e.g.:
  $\begin{Bmatrix} \text{*A Georges} \\ \text{Georges} \end{Bmatrix}$, j'ai connu la fille qui lui a écrit hier.

(v) The anaphor is clefted, e.g.:

$\left\{\begin{array}{l}\text{*De Marie} \\ \text{Marie}\end{array}\right\}$, c'est d'elle qu'ils ont parlé.

Cinque's arguments for this syntactic distinction are, in my opinion, convincing enough. The problem is, however, that given only the above features as a means of classifying particular instances of detachment constructions, there remains a large group of such constructions which cannot be assigned unambiguously to one type or the other. Namely, this group includes all lefthand NPs which do not happen to exhibit one of the above features, which are in fact very rare in actual discourse, as we shall see below. In her treatment of detachment structures in French, which essentially adopts Cinque's double source analysis of left detachments, Larsson (1979: 122) suggests a way of reducing somewhat this class of structures of ambiguous origin. Given her conclusion that right detachments, unlike their lefthand counterparts, appear to be all derived by a simple copying operation, she proposes that any lefthand element for which the corresponding righthand construction is grammatical be considered to be derived, or at least derivable, by transformation, while any lefthand detachment without a corresponding righthand structure be considered basic. Even if there were some argument for considering the former structures to be derived, and not just derivable, by transformation, this would still only solve the problem for a very restricted group of constructions, that is, essentially, lefthand NPs (or Pros) whose anaphor is an oblique argument of the verb, e.g.:

(7) Cette affaire, je préfère ne pas en parler.

since the comparable righthand structures are ungrammatical:

(8) *Je préfère ne pas en parler, cette affaire.[9]

Again, at least in the present corpus, the construction illustrated in (7) is relatively infrequent.

Given the lack of any distinguishing syntactic properties in most cases, one could ask whether there are other types of properties which might be correlated with the proposed syntactic distinction. In addition to the above-mentioned syntactic features, Cinque (1977) in fact hints at some intonational and pragmatic factors which appear to differentiate the two constructions. Unfortunately, the exact extent of Cinque's claims with respect to these properties is not clear, as his discussion of them is somewhat limited; however, the general lines of the hypothesis are clear enough.

What are these intonational and pragmatic properties? Cinque (1977: 406) suggests that the base-generated structure differs prosodically from the transformational one in that, with the former, "a much longer break intervenes between the lefthand NP and the rest of the S," and the NP "has a contour somewhat similar to that of questioned NPs." Pragmatically, Cinque describes the acceptable reading of these phonologically marked structures as the "*hanging topic* reading, to borrow a term of A. Grosu, since it exemplifies a construction that mainly serves to promote an NP to topic status at a point in the discourse when it was not a topic." Moreover, the anaphor of a hanging topic may convey new information, as when it is contrastive, while "a necessary condition for left dislocating an NP in Italian is that it be old information" (406).[10]

Galambos (1980: 130-31), in considering the pragmatics of left detachment constructions (she does not address their syntactic analysis), reiterates the distinction suggested by Cinque, describing a hanging topic as a topic which also functions as a "focus or center of attention," as indicated by a contrastive function or an accompanying emphatic element such as an 'apposition' or an interjection:

(9) a. Moi, je connais une brasserie... Toi, tu vas voir le patron.
   b. Mais moi, personnellement, j'en suis pas.
   c. Eh bien moi, j'attends tout simplement.

Galambos claims that these topics are "stressed", and "also accompanied by a rise in pitch and followed by a pause." On the other hand, what Galambos calls "topic-comment constructions par excellence" show none of these special prosodic features, as in:

(10) a. Les gens izz applaudissaient maman.
   b. Ca je m'en fous.

Thus, the preceding observations suggest a hypothesis whereby instances of the two proposed syntactic types of left detachment structures would be distinguishable by reference to certain pragmatic and/or phonological properties. To summarize, it is suggested that the following properties are associated with each type:

(a) BASE-GENERATED (Hanging Topic)
    (i) Emphatic/contrastive function
    (ii) Phonologically marked (pitch rise, pause)
    (iii) Referent becomes a topic, may be new to the discourse

(iv) May be accompanied by interjection or 'emphatic' adverbial expression
 (b) TRANSFORMATIONAL (Ordinary Topic)
   (i) Not emphatic or contrastive
   (ii) Phonologically unmarked
   (iii) Referent is already a topic
   (iv) No accompanying interjection or 'emphatic' adverbial expression

It is not entirely clear from Cinque's discussion what the intended relation is between these various properties. Note that, with the exception perhaps of number (iv), all of the properties of Ordinary Topics are defined negatively with respect to properties of Hanging Topics. The question is whether any of the properties of Hanging Topics may occur independently of the others. Cinque and Galambos seem to suggest that at least the first two always occur together, the pitch rise and pause being the phonological markers of the emphatic or contrastive function. Feature (iv) is clearly an optional lexical marker of this function. It is less apparent that the third property should necessarily be correlated with contrastive, or especially, with emphatic function, but we shall assume this as a working hypothesis, as we seek to confirm or discomfirm the preceding hypothesis by inspection of the corpus.

2.2. Pragmatic descriptions

There is little disagreement on the generalities of a pragmatic description of the left detachment constructions as in (1) above. All descriptions (Larsson 1979; Galambos 1980; Lambrecht 1981) consider them to be topic-comment structures, i.e. a way of overtly marking the articulation of a sentence into two parts, the first referring to what it is the sentence is about (topic), and the second expressing what the sentence has to say about that referent (comment). Thus, while the elements of ordinary sentences (without any detachments) may be described in terms of the topic and comment functions, it is only in left detachment (LD) constructions (and certain other similar constructions) that this distinction is overtly signalled.

The notion of topic itself requires some clarification, as the term has been used in various ways. Reinhart (1982) reviews the various uses of the term and argues for a notion of pragmatic aboutness, as opposed to the identification of topic with 'old information' or what is 'given'. While it is true that the topic of a particular sentence can only be identified relative to a particular context, Reinhart demonstrates that givenness is neither necessary nor sufficient for topichood.[11] According to Reinhart's definition of topic, which is adopted here, the sentence-topic is "the expression whose referent the sentence is about," in the sense that the assertion contained in the sentence is intended to expand our knowledge about the referent of that expression. Reinhart notes, for English, that LD is a structurally marked topic position, but points out that it is not the most reliable test for topichood in view of additional restrictions which apply to LDs. The test Reinhart suggests is to embed the sentence in an *about* sentence, e.g. (11b) shows *the book* to be the topic expression of (11a):

(11) a. Many more people are familiar with the book's classy title than are acquainted with its turgid text.

b. He said $\left\{\begin{array}{c}\text{about}\\ \text{of}\end{array}\right\}$ the book that many people are familiar with its classy title than are acquainted with its turgid text.

The preceding definition of topic entails a constraint on the comment portion of a LD structure to the effect that it must contain an assertion about the referent of the topic. Larsson (1979: 10), noting that LDs are possible in interrogatives, states that the comment gives some information or asks some question about the topic. Later in her discussion, Larsson notes that the existence of 'exceptional' cases where there is no anaphor of the LD in the accompanying clause, in fact necessitates the adoption of a less restrictive description of the topic-comment relation, such as that proposed by Dik (1978: 138): "For any pair of Theme T [i.e. topic] and Predication P [i.e. comment] to make sense, it must be relevant to pronounce P with respect to T." As Larsson (1979: 40) points out, this is a pragmatic rather than a simply semantic condition, since its satisfaction may depend on speakers' knowledge of the world.

Given that the preceding notion of topic is in fact defined in terms of the function of the comment portion of the sentence, the adoption of Dik's condition on the topic-comment relation will naturally entail a concomitant modification of the notion of topic. This question will be addressed below, in relation to the cases of LD with no anaphor. It remains that Reinhart's notion of topic is an adequate one for the 90% of the LDs of this corpus which do have an anaphor in the clause. (See sec. 6.2 for further discussion.)

Up to this point, I have described the topic-comment relation as an intrasentential relation. It has been observed, however, that the domain of a topic marked by LD may vary between the sentence and a larger segment of discourse. Lambrecht (1981: 2), for example, gives the following description of a LD construction: "The verb, followed or not by further constituents, represents together with the [anaphor of the left-detached expression] the comment or part of the comment if, as usual, the topic governs more than one clause." Galambos (1980: 126) is even more emphatic about the 'discourse-dependent' nature of the notion of topic, associating every instance of a topic-comment construction with the establishing of a new topic of discourse: "Once a topic-comment construction occurs, the topic is frequently sustained throughout a number of utterances by means of a coreferential pronoun, as well as by other more interesting devices. Thus, as long as the topic is maintained, no new topic-comment construction will occur." The latter is a strong form of the claim that LDs effect a shift in the topic of discourse, as noted for English by Keenan and Schieffelin (1976) and for Italian by Ochs and Duranti (1979).

Thus, another of the questions to be addressed in what follows is the level of topic to which the lefthand NP corresponds. If in fact it may be either a sentence-topic or a discourse-topic, we should like to know more precisely what is the relation between these two pragmatic functions, if in fact these should be conceived of as two separate functions.

3. THE DATA-GENERAL OBSERVATIONS AND HYPOTHESES

3.1. Preliminary observations

A summary of the types of LD constructions found in the corpus, according to the syntactic category of the lefthand element and the syntactic function of the anaphoric expression in the clause, is given in Table 1. These findings suggest the following observations:

(a) The type of LD construction claimed to be unambiguously tranformational in origin, i.e. where the lefthand element is a PP, is conspicuously absent from this corpus. In fact, just one example of that type was found, which is given in (12):

(12)   Même, même *à la corde à noeuds*, j'savais pas *y* monter.[12]

(II,37,9)

Clearly, such PP-detachments are of extremely limited frequency in the spoken language. It may be that such structures are characteristic of a more formal register, or it may be that they are infrequent in all registers because their pragmatic function requires a rather special context. Some further discussion of the function of these constructions may be found in section 3.3 below.

(b) The majority (62%) of the occurring LDs have a pronominal NP as the lefthand element. The question is, what are the consequences of this property with respect to the pragmatic function of the construction? Are these structures comparable, from a pragmatic point of view, to lexical NP detachments? From the point of view of the most general pragmatic description, the answer is a qualified yes, since in both cases the detached element usually represents the topic of the sentence, about which the accompanying clause makes a comment. However, in their more specific pragmatic aspects, the pronominal/lexical NP distinction clearly has significant consequences. It will be seen that certain LDs with *moi* require a modification of the definition of sentence-topic. Pronominal LDs will be examined in sections 4 and 6.2.

(c) In the case of both pronominal and lexical detachments, the large

ANAPHORIC EXPRESSION (Grammatical function)	DETACHED NOUN PHRASE (Type)					
	Pronominal		Lexical		Combined	
	No. of tokens	% of Pro	No. of tokens	% of NP	No. of tokens	% of total
Subject, total	525	82%	308	79%	835	81%
+Personal	410	64%	81*	21%	492	48%
1 sg. Other	364 46	57% 7%				
−Personal (c'/ça)	115	18%	227*	58%	343	33%
D.O.	27	4%	26	7%	52	5%
I.O.	14	2%	6	2%	21	2%
Oblique	6	1%	4	1%	10	1%
Poss. Det., total	11	2%	0	0%	11	1%
1 sg.	9					
No anaphor, total	61	9%	45	12%	106	10%
moi...	41	6%				
nous...	10					
ça...	9					
Total	644		389		1033	

* refers to the number of tokens with a pronominal anaphor of the +Personal or −Personal type.

Table 1

majority of the constructions (82% and 79% respectively) have anaphors which are the grammatical subject of the accompanying clause. Moreover, of the remaining 19%, 10% have no anaphor in the clause, so LDs with nonsubject anaphors account for only 9% of the total. This would seem to contradict Lambrecht's (1981: 52) claim that detached NPs "often correspond not to former subjects but to objects", though I do not believe this detracts from Lambrecht's main point, i.e. that detached NPs are essentially "pragmatically determined entities". The relative frequency of subjects with LDs appears to be quite high: I have counted a total of 165 lexical NP subjects without LDs where a detachment would not have violated a pragmatic or syntactic constraint.[13] Comparing this number to the 310 lexical subjects which are detached, only about one-third of lexical subjects are not detached. However, the facts of (d) suggest a qualification to this view.

(d) Within the category of lexical NP-detachments with subject anaphors, the majority (74%) have as their anaphor nonpersonal *c-* (elided *ce* in *c'est*) or *ça*, rather than *il(s)/elle(s)*. The higher relative frequency of LD with *ce/ça* than with *il(s)/elle(s)* is indicated by the following observation: examination of 'nondetached' (i.e. ordinary lexical) subject NPs with the verb *être* reveals that the overwhelming majority of these have *il(s)/elle(s)* and not *c-* as an appropriate anaphor. In other words, with the verb *être*, LD is quasi-obligatory just in case the subject NP has *c-* as an appropriate anaphor. This suggests that a more meaningful comparison than the one between nondetached lexical subjects and total detached lexical subjects is that between nondetached lexical subjects (165) and detached lexical subjects with *il/elle*, of which there are only 81. In other words, if we disregard LDs with *ce/ça* anaphors, on the grounds that these are grammaticalized, only about one-third of the NP-subjects which could be detached are so. This difference in behavior according to the subject anaphor poses problems for the analysis which sees subject LDs (specifically, the clitic anaphor) as primarily a new means of marking subject agreement, following the loss of the postverbal inflections. (Cf. Wartburg 1946: 61).

(e) Within the category of pronominal detachments with subject anaphors, the majority (69%) of the occurring constructions are with the first-person singular *moi*. This contrasts with Keenan and Schieffelin's (1976) study of LD in English, where only one (2%) of the LDs of their corpus makes direct reference to the speaker or hearer (246). Apparently, at least some LDs in French have some function or functions which are in some respects distinct from those of structurally similar constructions in English.

(f) Finally, it is of interest that approximately 10% of the total LDs are ones where the detached element has no corresponding anaphoric expression in the clause. It seems to me that this proportion is a bit higher than one would expect, given Larsson's (1979) description of such cases as 'exceptional'. Such constructions are about equally frequent with pronominal and lexical detachments. These constructions and their implications for the description of the topic-comment relation are considered in section 6.2.

3.2. Problems with the syntactic-pragmatic correlation hypothesis

In sec. 2.1 above, I outlined the syntactic-pragmatic correlation hypothesis (SPCH) suggested in Cinque (1977), which posits a pragmatic distinction between the phonologically marked Hanging Topic (HT) and the unmarked Ordinary Topic (OT). The HT is characterized by special pragmatic motivation (contrast or emphasis), while the OT has no such special motivation.

While the foregoing hypothesis is initially appealing, it is in fact fraught with difficulties, with respect both to the correlation between syntax and pragmatics, and to the proposed pragmatic distinction itself. First of all, it is not clear why there should be such a correlation between base generation and special pragmatic motivation on the one hand, and between transformational derivation and lack of such motivation on the other. In fact, in recent years some linguists have argued that the existence of certain generally accepted tranformational rules may be explained by the pragmatic work which they accomplish. Moreover, the pragmatic analysis of PP-detachments proposed by Lambrecht (1981: 67-72) is exactly the opposite of what Cinque's hypothesis would predict: according to the latter, these are clear cases of transformational LDs, and yet they are, according to Lambrecht, essentially contrastive in function.

A second and major problem, with regard to the pragmatic distinction itself, is that the SPCH suggests a categorical correlation between phonological features, pragmatic function, and information status of the LD-referent (i.e. new to the discourse, 'old information', etc.), while these three properties are in fact independent of each other. This can be seen by examining detachments from the corpus.

3.2.1. *LD in contrastive contexts*

Consider (13). (In this section, pitch rises will be marked 1, 2, or 3 corresponding to my approximate perception of three different levels of relative pitch rise, 3 being the highest level.)

(13) Moi je trouve que *la cuisine* ↗2 c'est l'endroit le plus important d'une maison. (I,10,7)

The context of (13) excludes any contrastive interpretation of this LD. The intonation and stress pattern of the LD is typical of noncontrastive left-detached NPs: *cuisine* shows a moderate pitch rise, just slightly higher than the pitch level of a non-detached subject NP, and it is followed by a very slight pause.

The LDs of (14) are prime candidates for HTs; they are clearly contrastive in function and, though the pitch levels of the LDs are not significantly higher than that of the preceding example, the LDs are marked by extra stress, a property Galambos (1980: 131) associates with the HT:

(14) *les yo*↗2**gourts** *c'*est, *c'*est les, *c'*est plus liquide et le, *les ya*↗2**ourts** *c'*est plus solide. (II,62,2)

However, there clearly is special motivation in this case for extra emphasis on the detached NPs, inasmuch as the current discourse-topic is precisely the existence of two different words for 'yogurt'; thus the phonetic difference between the two is naturally stressed.

Example (15) is more typical of the use of LDs in a contrastive context. The previous discourse-topic is cranberries and the French word for them. (The speakers have just been shown some cranberry sauce.) The speaker thinks she has discovered the French equivalent in the word *goyavier* 'guava'.

(15) M: Alors *les goyaviers* ↗3 *c'*est un fruit extrêmement doux qui fond sous la langue, et *celui-là il* ↗2 a l'air bien dur, j'l'ai touché, qui fond sous la langue et on fait une liqueur avec et j'en ai à la maison, de la liqueur de goyavier, qu'on a importée et euh, qui est excellente. Mais alors *ça ça* ↗2 a l'air plus dur, hein.
(E: Oui, sinon?)
M: *Le goyavier* ↗3 euh, *le fruit auquel je pense*, *c'*est un fruit ↗2 (?)
  (I,14,16-18)

None of the LDs of (15) carry any extra emphatic stress. As to pitch, the lefthand NPs *les goyaviers* and *le goyavier* show a rise somewhat higher than in the noncontrastive (13), but the lefthand pronouns *celui-là* and *ça* are marked by more moderate rises.

In the following, contrastive LDs show pitch levels lower than or equivalent to that of the noncontrastive LD of (13):

(16) (Previous discourse-topic (DT) is the problem of obesity in America)
M: Puis alors, c'est tellement facile avec tous ces fast foods. Enfin, t'es, t'es dans une rue et y en a deux. Regarde à Dinkytown combien y en a.

↗2   ↗1
C: Oui, *nous* c'est les cafés, *eux* c'est les fast foods.
B: Oui.

↗2   ↗2
C: Alors *nous les cafés* bon, un café
M: En principe, voilà, un café

↗2
C: Un petit ballon, à la rigueur, mais, mais *les fast foods* (c'est) des frites, des cheeseburgers, c'est même pas du cheese qu'i'mettent   (II,56,7-12)

Notice that within each discourse segment represented in (15) and (16), the lowest pitch rises occur on pronominal rather than lexical NP detachments.

To summarize thus far, it is apparent that contrastive LDs are not necessarily marked by a relatively higher pitch rise. Rather, observed intonation contours may be described as including a minimal rise, an intermediate rise comparable to that of noncontrastive NP LDs, and a somewhat greater rise, but which is still not ordinarily accompanied by extra stress. A factor which apparently correlates with differences in pitch level is pronominal vs. lexical NP status of the LD. Another factor may be position of the LD with respect to turn boundaries: e.g. in (15), the more marked LDs are both turn-initial. Neither is the presence of a following pause a correlate of contrastive function. Contrastive LDs sometimes show no pause at all, and the principal cases of clearly observable pauses are those where there intervenes some hesitation particle or interjection such as *euh*, *bon*, etc.

Recall that the SPCH implies that referents of contrastive LDs are not topics prior to their occurrence in the LD. Examples (15) and (16) show this correlation to be invalid. In fact, the typical case, in explicitly contrastive contexts such as the above, is that where the objects of comparison are already topics of the discourse. (See sec. 5.2.2 for further discussion.)

3.2.2. *Introduction of new referents*

It appears that there is some lack of clarity in Cinque's use of the term *contrastive* referring to the HT, since he refers the reader, for a more detailed pragmatic analysis of this construction, to Keenan and Schieffelin (1976), whose description of the functions of LD in English in fact covers a much broader range of functions than what is usually understood by 'contrastive'. For instance, (17) illustrates Keenan and Schieffelin's 'alternative referent' function, which is a particular case of the more general function of topic shift:

(17) nous je sais qu'on se prive pas, hein, au point de vue viande euh,
↗2+
les légumes, bon euh, évidemment c'est parfois (?) (I,26,10)

Though the context does not suggest as explicit a contrast or comparison as in the preceding examples, *légumes* is related to the previous discourse-topic, *viande*, in such a way that we may call this LD contrastive in a broad sense, or better, perhaps, 'comparative' (cf. sec.3.3). Notice that *légumes* is here introduced into the discourse for the first time. In fact, a significant number of the LDs which are phonologically marked by higher pitch rises (and often followed by hesitation particles) cannot be construed as contrastive in any sense, or as satisfying one of Keenan and Schieffelin's functions; rather, their markedness must be attributed to the fact that they introduce referents which are new to the discourse, as in (18)-(20):

↗2+
(18) *la femme* euh elle m'a donné euh, comment on appelle ça euh
(I,39,14)

In (18) the discourse-topic is the speaker's job as a teacher in a cooking school and how she got the job; the NP *la femme*, first mentioned here, apparently refers to the woman in charge of the school.

↗2+
(19) Enfin c'était en euh, *Nancy elle* aimerait beaucoup ça (II,71,6)

In (19) the discourse-topic is the film 'Madame Rosa' and the fact that it has a lot of slang; Nancy, first mentioned here, is a mutual friend who is particularly interested in slang.

Example (20) is particularly interesting; it includes three dislocations of the same, coreferent NP, each of which shows, I think, a different level of pitch, corresponding to a different pragmatic context. C's utterance overlaps the middle of M's turn, the overlapping being indicated by brackets. The first two instances of the LD are in C's utterance, the third in M's. The discourse-topic is plans for attending a play, for which special ticket prices are available for groups.

(20) M: y a Beth qui veut y aller, euh, y a [(?) y a Jean-Marc, y a moi,
↗2
bon] hein, *Georges i*'veut pas y aller
↗3   ↗1
C: [*Georges i*'n'y va pas, *Georges i*'veut pas y aller]   (II,18,4)

Note that the first occurrence of *Georges* has the relatively high pitch characteristic of new NPs; the second shows a minimal rise, inasmuch as the referent is no longer new; the pitch level of the third occurrence is intermediate with respect to the preceding two instances, which is explained by the fact that the referent is not new, but, in contrast to the second instance, it is now placed in the contrastive context which is set up by M's enumeration of other people wanting to go.

It appears then that referents which are 'new to the discourse' show more consistent phonological marking than do those in contrastive contexts. Once again, however, there is no *necessary* correlation between phonological marking and the status 'new to the discourse'. Each of the following LDs represent the first mention of the LD-referent, yet the pitch rise is moderate, and there is no pause (or hesitation marker):

(21) (DT = the swimming test of the baccalaureat exam.)
M: ... Non non, on est obligé de plonger.
↗2   (↗3)
C: On était obligé, *le mec il* m'a poussée!   (II,38,14)

(22) (DT = silly answers given by their students on quizzes.)
↗2
L'année dernière, en 1101, on m'a dit que, *les colonies d'vacances c*'étaient pour les hommes politiques.   (II,27,4)

Such cases as (21) and (22) violate the supposed condition on OTs (i.e. phonologically unmarked LDs) that the referent is always 'old information'.[14]

It is evident that the particular pragmatic distinction proposed in the SPCH is without empirical validity, at least for French. Contrastive LDs do not necessarily carry special phonological marking, and, with respect to information statuses, their referents, like those of noncontrastive LDs, show the full range of possibilities, including new to the discourse, 'old information', and already topical (cf. sec. 5.2.2). We have seen that phonological marking often accompanies the introduction of a new referent, but these cases are not necessarily contrastive nor emphatic. High pitch may also serve an emphatic function (which may occur in contrastive as well as noncontrastive contexts), and the latter is independent of the information status of the referent. For instance, emphatic stress was seen with already topical referents (in a comparative context) in (14) above; an example of emphatic stress with a new referent may be found in (121) of sec. 5.4.[15]

3.3. Contrastiveness and topic shift

We noted in the preceding section a certain ambiguity in the use of the term *contrastive*, and also alluded to Keenan and Schieffelin's (1976) description of English LD functions as a very broad notion of contrastiveness. Given the importance of this function with respect to LD in French as well, I think a brief digression to clarify this notion is warranted.

Probably the best-defined notion of contrastiveness is Chafe's (1976) description, according to which a sentence such as **Ron**ald *made the hamburgers* (with emphatic stress on *Ronald*) is contrastive inasmuch as it satisfies the following conditions: (1) existence of presupposed knowledge about some state of affairs ('someone (X) made hamburgers'); (2) knowledge of a set of possible candidates for involvement in that state of affairs (Ronald, y, z...); and (3) the assertion of which candidate is in fact the correct one (X = Ronald). Lambrecht (1981: 67-71) takes up this description of contrastiveness but further designates it as *emphatic* contrastiveness, or simply 'emphasis', which he distinguishes from nonemphatic contrastiveness. Following Chafe, emphatic contrastiveness involves a negative connotation; i.e. in asserting which is the correct candidate, it is also asserted that the other possible candidates are *not* correct, so that a test for this type of contrastiveness is the possibility of insertion of the phrase "rather than (instead of, not) [...]" after the focus of contrast. On the basis of this test, Lambrecht distinguishes the following two sentence-types:

(23) a. A Pierre j-ui donnerai un livre.
 b. C-est à **Pierre** qu-j-donnerai un livre.

The cleft construction of (23b) is emphatic, inasmuch as the focussed PP *à Pierre* may be followed by *plutôt qu'à Paul*; here *à Pierre* also carries the more marked emhatic stress. The left-detached PP of (23a), on the other hand, is not emphatic but only contrastive, in Lambrecht's terms, as it does not satisfy the same test for negative connotation.

Lambrecht maintains that sentences having a lefthand PP, as in (23a) above, are inherently contrastive, basing this claim on the association of contrastiveness and the presence of case marking: "if a 'focus of contrast' involves assertion of which of the possible candidates for some given action is the right one, it follows that the semantic role of this candidate must already have been established with respect to that action" (68). Thus, inherently contrastive PP-detachments are distinguished from ordinary topic-comment structures which show no case marking (e.g. *Pierre j-ui donnerai un livre*). But this distinction between noncontrastive topic-comment constructions and (nonemphatic) contrastive constructions of course runs into the same difficulties as those encountered by the attempt to distinguish on formal grounds two syntactic types of LD: since subject and object NPs carry no case marking, the two types of constructions are formally indistinguishable where the lefth- and NP is coreferent with the subject or direct object. In such cases, Lambrecht points to the immediate linguistic context as indicating the appropriateness of a contrastive interpretation.

Interestingly, in concluding his discussion, Lambrecht notes that the lack of a consistent formal distinction between the contrastive and noncontrastive detachment constructions is parallelled by an apparent functional similarity between the two construction types, which "may have to do with the notion of topic shift" (72).

What I would like to emphasize here is precisely the close relation that exists between the functions of contrast and topic shift. In fact, contrastive LDs could be seen as simply a special case of topic shift. To underline the relatedness of these two functions, I prefer to use the term 'comparative' in place of Lambrecht's "nonemphatic contrastive". In fact, many LDs which introduce a new topic can be described as comparative in function due to the nature of topic development in free conversation. That is, the new topic is usually related in some way to the previous topic; this relatedness often is such that the current and the previous topic are both particular examples of some more general class of entities, or they are both involved in some general phenomenon, which constitutes the larger discourse-topic. Here I am borrowing the language of Keenan and Schieffelin's (1976) description of LD in English. According to the latter, the major specific functions of English LDs, or "Referent + Proposition" constructions, are the introduction of an alternative referent with respect to one previously specified with respect to some predication, or the introduction of a particular case of some general phenomenon under discussion, or of a particular member of a previously specified set (244). These functions include that of contrast but are broader than what is usually implied by that term. In particular, Keenan and Schieffelin point out that this description differs from that of Chafe (1976), for example, in that the referent introduced may not have been already entertained by the hearer as a viable alternative.

What I call a 'comparative' context, then, in fact subsumes a variety of particular types of contexts, ranging from the explicitly contrastive context to that usually described in terms of topic shift. In the first type, both terms of the comparison (i.e. expressions referring to these entities) tend to occur very near each other in the discourse, usually in the same turn of the same speaker, and there is often a high degree of structural similarity in the containing utterances (as in (14) and (16) above). In the 'topic shift' type of comparative context, the two terms of the comparison may be separated by a number of intervening turns and typically (though not necessarily) occur in turns of different speakers (as in (17) and (20)). In other words, the first type might be seen as an explicit comparison, while the second may be only implicitly comparative. Examples from the corpus may be seen as ranging along a continuum of comparativeness having these two types of contexts as endpoints.

It is interesting to compare examples of comparative LDs from this corpus with examples cited by Keenan and Schieffelin (1976) in their discussion of LD in English. Though the pragmatic description they propose fits the French data very well, there is a perceivable difference in the two sets of data; namely, a number of the French examples are much closer to the explicitly comparative context type than are the English examples, which generally correspond to the 'topic shift' type. This probably reflects the fact that LD is generally more prevalent in French than in English, and is readily used where the referent is already evoked or even a topic of the discourse. In English, on the other hand, the primary function of LD is apparently to introduce a referent which is not already in the foreground.

There is phonological evidence for this difference in function, or rather for the greater diversity of functions of LD in French: Keenan and Schieffelin note that in English, the LD "is often followed by a pause or by a hesitation marker (e.g. uhh)", which is not at all the rule in French, except when the LD introduces a referent which is new to the discourse (cf. sec. 3.2 above). It may appear that I am echoing Cinque's (1977) hypothesis that French and English differ in that French has both transformational LDs and base-generated hanging topics, while English has only the latter. While the present data do not support, as shown above (sec. 3.2), the particular pragmatic and phonological correlates of the syntactic distinction proposed in Cinque (1977), they do support the view that LD in French has the same functions as LD in English plus additional functions not shared by the English construction. This question will be further addressed in sec. 7 below.

3.4. A new hypothesis — In search of LDs of minimal pragmatic motivation

What might be retained from the SPCH, apart from the question of syntactic origin, is the possibility of drawing distinctions among LD-types with respect to the nature and degree of pragmatic motivation. The question of degree of pragmatic motivation is significant in relation to the question of the grammaticalization of the LD structure which some have suggested is taking place with respect to subjects. That is, the subject clitic coreferent with the LD is seen as an obligatory agreement marker, taking up the function of the post-verbal inflections which are no longer realized in the spoken language (cf. Wartburg 1946: 61). If this explanation is correct, and the left detachment of subjects is, or is becoming, essentially a grammatical phenomenon, then we would expect to find a certain number of instances of LD with little or no pragmatic motivation, i.e. resembling Cinque's Ordinary Topic or Galambos' "topic-comment construction par excellence".

The notion of pragmatic motivation calls for some discussion. In relation to Cinque's hypothesis, I have used the expression '*special* pragmatic motivation', since the kind of motivation in question was limited to the most transparently pragmatic functions, i.e. contrast, emphasis, or introduction of a referent which is new to the discourse. But there are of course other, less transparent types of pragmatic motivation. We will consider some of these in the following sections as we look at particular types of LD constructions.

Likely candidates for LDs of minimal pragmatic motivation would be those LDs which are phonologically least marked, which apear to be the *moi je* type, and those which are quasi-obligatory, i.e. the NP *c'est* type. We shall see below that the former clearly fall within the category of pragmatically motivated; though the function of the latter is not so obviously pragmatic in nature, I will argue that the apparent grammaticalization of LD in this context may be explained by the combination of the pragmatic properties of LD and semantic properties of *c'est*.

The principal remaining cases of LD with subject anaphors are those with detached NP and subject pronouns *il(s)/elle(s)*. Interestingly, the majority of these cases can be interpreted as having one of the transparently pragmatic functions referred to above, i.e. comparison, emphasis, or introduction of a new referent. Cases where one of these descriptions is not plausible account for only about one-fourth of the LDs of this type.

Of course, one could argue that any acceptable dislocation of a subject is necessarily pragmatically motivated, inasmuch as it would appear to automatically satisfy the topic-comment relation, by virtue of the nature of the subject-predicate relation. This would be, in other words, the minimal degree of pragmatic motivation. However, there is at least one important difference between the subject-predicate relation and the topic-comment relation, in addition to the recoverability and referentiality conditions on topics. Namely, it is generally assumed that a comment makes an assertion (or, in the case of interrogatives, requests information) about the topic. Thus, a clear candidate for an LD of minimal pragmatic motivation would be one which occurs in a subordinate, nonasserted clause. The corpus contains a small number of such examples, e.g.:

(24) a. tu sais les énormes bottes comme *Jean-Marc il* a (II,14,7)
b. j'avais un philosophe, un type dont *la matière principale c*'est la philosophie (I,52,4)
c. (Discourse topic is a particular type of pastry that the speaker's mother always bought for her children when they were sick) l'faut pas les commander parce que comme *ma maman* (euh) elle devait pas prévoir qu'on allait être malade, euh

(III,51,16)

(24b) is of course an instance of the *NP c'est* structure; note that the description I will give of the pragmatic motivation of NP *c'est* does not require that the clause be asserted. Likewise, it seems to me that the function of introducing a new referent may apply whether or not the clause is asserted, so that the LD of (24a) might be explained in that way. A handful of cases like (24c) still remain where neither of these explanations applies. (Note however, in (24c), the presence of the hesitation particle *euh*, which favors the subsequent occurrence of the clitic pronoun.)

Lambrecht (1984a) proposes a pragmatic explanation which would apply to any subject LD (but only without the further qualification noted below). According to his analysis, LD is one of several different constructions which have the effect of allowing utterances to conform to a pragmatic constraint on spoken French subjects which specifies that the latter must be both topics and given (in the sense of Chafe (1976), i.e. which can be assumed to be present in the mind of the addressee at the moment of the utterance). Whether or not this particular analysis is correct, notice that the notion that any subject LD is inherently pragmatically motivated leads to the question of why all subjects are not dislocated (cf. sec. 3.1 above). Lambrecht (1984b) suggests an answer which is, to a large extent, corroborated by this data, namely, that LD tends to occur in foregrounded and not in backgrounded parts of the discourse. An alternative (but not entirely equivalent formulation — cf. sec. 5.2.4) is that LD tends to occur only with referents which have the status of a topic of the discourse. Although the usefulness and validity of this claim will be further examined in sec. 3.6.2 and 5.2.4, I would note here that the LDs of (24) above are counterexamples to the proposed constraint, since none of their referents can be said to be discourse-topics.

The questions raised here will be addressed in more detail in subsequent sections dealing with particular types of LD constructions, and finally, in the Conclusion.

3.5. Alternative syntactic analyses

Though our primary concern is with the pragmatics of detachment constructions, a few remarks concerning the syntactic problem raised in 2.1 above are appropriate. We have seen above (section 3.2) that the hypothesized correlation between phonological markedness and special pragmatic function, specifically contrastiveness, is disconfirmed by the data. Though intuitively there may be a certain appeal in the association of transformational origin and phonological and pragmatic unmarkedness, it is sufficient to point to the frequent construction type exemplified by *moi c'est pareil* for its falsification: the *moi*-LD is typically quite unmarked, but the absence of an anaphor in the clause excludes a transformational origin.

An alternative approach would be to start from the original assumption that PP-detachments are transformational, together with Lambrecht's observations concerning the contrastive function of PP-detachments (see above), and propose that other detachments which can be argued to have a similar contrastive function are also generated by transformation. However, I think the preceding discussion of contrastiveness and topic shift has shown that any attempt to delimit two distinct classes of contrastive vs. noncontrastive LDs is bound to fail, without giving some more precise but necessarily arbitrary content to the notion of contrastive environment.

It appears then that in the case of detachment constructions, pragmatic properties offer no help in confirming the validity of the proposed syntactic distinction. If one accepts that there are two possible syntactic origins, there remains the derivational ambiguity of a large class of LD constructions. What appears to be the only nonarbitrary conclusion is the one suggested by Larsson to the effect that any left detachment which would be grammatical as a right detachment either is or may be transformationally derived. Such an analysis is supported by the facts of coreference noted by Deulofeu (1979), namely, that it is only in PP-detachments that coreference between the detached element and an anaphor contained in the accompanying clause is obligatory. If such coreference occurs in the case of a NP-detachment, it is the result of rules of discourse coherence, and not of morphosyntactic relations. For example, (25a) and (25b):

(25) a. à mon père je lui parle
b. mon père je lui parle

differ, according to Deulofeu, in that *mon père* and *lui* may be disreferent in (b) but not in (a). This is demonstrated by the acceptability, given the appropriate context, of an utterance such as (26):

(26) mon père je parle à Paul

which Deulofeu suggests may be interpreted as, for instance, "en présence de mon père, je parle à Paul" (100). For Deulofeu, cases of NP-detachments where the potential anaphor shows no case marking (i.e. with subject or direct object clitics) are ambiguous between the coreferent and disreferent readings, representing "un cryptotype syntaxique du français".

Accepting the difference in coreference between left-detached PPs and NPs noted by Deulofeu, an analysis whereby only the PP-detachments are derived by transformation seems preferable. As for nominal detachments, I believe that the facts of this corpus will show that these are essentially a pragmatic phenomenon, inasmuch as the majority of these constructions have a strong pragmatic motivation. Moreover, while there is considerable diversity of particular pragmatic functions, there is at the same time a basic pragmatic unity characterizing all instances of LD, which argues against any attempt to distinguish various syntactic types of LD based on pragmatic properties.

3.6. The 'domain' of LD: sentence-topic and discourse-topic

In section 2.2 above, I cited previous descriptions of LD in French which emphasize the LD function of establishing an NP as a topic which is usually maintained through more than one utterance, i.e. as a discourse-topic as well as a sentence-topic. It is this function which has been referred to as 'topic shift'. In this section, I will attempt to clarify the role of LD with respect to sentence-topic (ST) and discourse-topic (DT), and in order to do so will first try to give some precise content to the notion of DT. Both this notion and the role of LD with respect to DT is considerably more complex than the previous literature would lead one to believe. In particular, I will argue that an accurate description of the thematic structure of discourse, and, consequently, of the function of LD, requires a multi-level notion of topic.

3.6.1. *The notion of discourse-topic*

A DT is, roughly, that thing which a segment of discourse larger than the sentence is about, i.e. about which it supplies information. Some formulations require that the DT take the form of a proposition; e.g. van Dijk (1977: 136) defines the topic of a discourse as "a proposition entailed by the joint set of propositions expressed by the sequence". We agree, however, with Reinhart (1982) that the DT may be an entity as well as a proposition.

DT-hood is often indicated by the occurrence in successive sentences of anaphoric expressions referring to the given entity, or, less frequently, the given proposition. This syntactic indication, however, is neither necessary nor sufficient. Though there is no simple syntactic test for DT, given its suprasentential scope, the notion is perhaps intuitively clearer than that of ST. Along with the requirement of suprasentential scope, I propose a pragmatic criterion similar to Reinhart's (1982) criterion for ST (see sec. 2.2), namely that the given stretch of discourse is understood as intending to expand our knowledge (or more precisely, the discourse participants' knowledge) of the entity or proposition which is the DT.

In contrast to van Dijk's view of DTs as propositional, Lambrecht (1981) and Galambos (1980) implicitly suggest a view of topic as restricted to entities. Notice that, at the sentence level, the identification of the topic corresponds to the segmentation of the sentence into a topic portion and a comment portion. Lambrecht's (1981: 2) discussion suggests that the same kind of segmentation is possible at the level of DT, which would only be the case if the DT were explicitly represented by an expression in the discourse. One could perhaps argue for a notion of DT including only entities, if the set of

DTs were defined simply as the set of all the STs of the discourse. However, a much more revealing notion of DT is one which incorporates, at this higher level, the same 'informational purpose' criterion as is applied at the sentence level.

An example from the corpus will help to clarify the difference between these two competing notions of DT, and will serve as empirical justification for choosing the second of these. In addition, the example will show why our notion of DT must allow the contemporaneous existence of several DTs at various levels corresponding to increasingly longer stretches of the discourse. That is, in this type of discourse, it is not usually the case that a new topic simply supplants the previous one; rather, new topics tend to be 'embedded' in a more general topic. I will refer to these various levels of DT, as necessary, as DT", DT', and DT.

Consider the following discourse segment:

(27) C: (looking at a picture in a National Wildlife magazine)
Ca c'est rigolo alors.
M: Qu'est-ce que c'est?
C: Un oiseau, tu sais, tu sais que *les animaux*, quand ils sentent qu'i'vont être euh, qu'y a le, l'oiseau de proie ou quoi que ce soit qui vient, qui les prend pour les manger, ils ont une certaine défense quoi, plus ou moins. Alors y en a, *le putois*, il y a l'odeur, etc. Et regarde cet oiseau. Il se gonfle et il fait peur au
M: Oh. Il est vu de, de dos ou de, face?
E&C: Non non, de face. (I,19,16-20)

If we look simply at the succession of STs (whether or not the expression is detached), we have first, in the first two turns, the picture C. is looking at; then, in the third turn, *les animaux*, followed by *le putois* ('skunk'), and finally, in the last sentence of this turn and in the following turns, the bird in the picture. The DT of this entire segment, or the DT", is a proposition such as "The thing in this picture is a bird in a defensive posture", since the purpose of the entire segment is to identify the object in the photo. The lowest-level DT covers the part of the text from *tu sais* through the sentence about skunks; this DT is the proposition "Animals have certain defenses", which serves as an explanation with respect to the DT'. The sentence about skunks, in turn, serves as a particular case illustrating the preceding propositional DT (*le putois* being a ST but not a DT).

Considering the two competing notions of DT, notice that a description that simply lists the various STs of this excerpt and calls them topics of the discourse fails to capture the functional relations existing between these referents (and the accompanying predications) in the discourse. Notice that, with respect to the part of the discourse covered by the DT "Animals have certain defenses", such a description would fail to capture the difference between this discourse and another possible one where the entity referred to by *les animaux* is the DT; that is, in the latter case, one would expect the subsequent utterances to go on to enumerate other properties of animals.

We have been assuming so far that there is reason to distinguish ST and DT. The positing of multiple levels of DT suggests that perhaps this distinction is not necessary, and that ST is simply the lowest level of DT. It is true that in some cases the ST/DT distinction appears to be quite arbitrary, being based only on length of the discourse segment. However, there are at least two reasons for maintaining the distinction. First, the ST differs from the DT in that it must be explicitly represented in the sentence; i.e. a ST corresponds to some expression of the sentence. Thus, as suggested above, it is only at the sentence-level that topic-comment organization is necessarily describable in structural terms.

The second reason for maintaining the ST/DT distinction has to do with the relative importance of a referent outside of the sentence in which it occurs. That is, there is a trivial sense of 'discourse-topic' according to which any ST is also necessarily a topic of the discourse in which it occurs. However, though every sentence presumably has a topic, STs differ with respect to their prominence in the discourse as a whole. Essential to the concept of DT is the notion that the referent has a prominence which goes beyond the sentence in which it occurs.

To reiterate the point of example (27), the problem with a description such as that of Galambos (1980) which suggests a one-to-one correspondence between LDs and DTs is that, assuming the above-mentioned 'informational purpose' criterion for DTs, such a description fails to recognize that the DT often takes the form of a proposition, of which the LD-expression is simply one argument. The source of this difficulty is no doubt a certain imprecision in the use of the term 'discourse-topic'. What Galambos and others apparently mean by 'discourse-topic' is simply a referent which figures in, or is prominent in, a segment of discourse longer than the sentence. It may well be that such a concept is necessary, in this case as well as in linguistic decription in general, but it should be assigned some name other than 'discourse-topic', such as, for example, 'discourse entity'. The set of discourse entities would no doubt include (without being limited to) those referents which are subjects of any propositional DTs.

3.6.2. *LD, sentence-topic, and discourse-topic in the corpus*

The first observation to be made is that the large majority (at least about 90%) of the LDs of the corpus do represent STs, following Reinhart's notion of ST. LDs with subject anaphors are of course unproblematic in this respect, and the 9% with nonsubject anaphors also satisfy the pragmatic 'aboutness' criterion (see sec. 5.3). There are some problematic cases, however, among the LDs with no anaphor in the clause; we will see in sec. 6.2 that these require an extension of the notion of ST to include what Chafe (1976) refers to as 'Chinese-style topics'.[16]

The next question is that of the status of LDs and DT. Here, both possible cases obtain; i.e. a left-detached expression may be a DT as well as a ST, or it may be only a ST and not a DT. Cases of the first type, where it is both ST and DT, coincide with cases of DT referring to entities rather than propositions.

An example of the coincidence of ST and DT is given in (28). The general topic or DT' of the larger discourse segment from which this excerpt is taken, is saunas. In what precedes this excerpt, E. and M. have been referring to two different types of sauna, the 'true' sauna and the American or swimming-pool sauna, without making the difference explicit.

(28) M: [...] parce que j'ai trouvé un vrai.
E: Non, mais ça fait du bien, quand tu as nagé.
C: Pourquoi? Qu'est-ce qu'y a? C'est quoi le vrai?
M: Ah *le vrai sauna*, c'est magnifique, c'est magnifique. Tu rentres là-dedans, bon tu y vas pour trois, quatre heures, quand tu ressors, tu as l'impression d'avoir une nouvelle peau. Alors, c'est, c'est, le, le système un peu du sauna des piscines, mais y a tellement, y a tellement de vapeur, que tu ne vois pas ton voisin, pratiquement, que tu marches dans l'noir, c'est assez impressionnant et puis alors, constamment, y a comme des, des petites rivières, des petits ruisseaux d'eau qui se renouvellent. (II,5,2-11)

Le vrai sauna is both the topic of its sentence, and the DT of the whole segment beginning with its occurrence and continuing beyond what is shown here, since the subsequent utterances all serve the purpose of describing the true sauna.

As to the second case, where the left-dislocated element corresponds to the ST but is not a DT, the noncoincidence of ST and DT may be attributed to various specific factors. In what follows, I shall enumerate and illustrate various types of cases found in the data.

The first cases we shall consider are those where the distinction between ST and DT appears somewhat arbitrary, in that the referent of the LD appears to have the same status as other DTs in the immediate context, but does not qualify as DT simply because this topic did not happen to be continued by the speaker or another participant, for somewhat arbitrary reasons, i.e. because a competing topic was taken up instead. An example is given in (29), part of a discourse about various Protestant sects:

(29) E: Ah moi j'trouve que les protestants sont bien plus stricts.
B: Oui, mais y a quand même des degrés de protestants aussi.
E: Oui, c'est ça. C'est comme les, *les Baptistes* euh, c'est un, c'est, ça va, c'est plutôt des protestants, eh bien, alors là, les Baptistes, hein, c'est que
M: Moi, le le *le luthérianisme*, *le luthérianisme*, de ma connaissance, c'est libéral.
E: ils sont, il faut s'accrocher, hein, les Baptistes ici, j'ai rencontré une famille, oh la la!
C: Oui.
M: Et alors *les Mormons*, qu'est-ce que c'est?
E: Ah ben ça, c'est encore autre chose. (I,71,5-12)

The LD which does not qualify as a DT is *le luthérianisme*, since it is limited to this sentence. Notice that *le luthérianisme* is one of several names of religious sects mentioned here, and that, functionally, it seems to be on a par with these other NPs (*les Baptistes*, *les Mormons*) which *are* DTs. Cases of this type account for a relatively small proportion of the total cases of noncoincidence of ST and DT.

For the majority of LDs which do not qualify as DTs, the referent fails with respect to both criteria for DT. That is, not only is the referent not referred to in succeeding sentences, but it also fails the 'informational purpose' criterion, in that it is functionally subordinate to the current DT. In other words, in contrast to the type just examined, these cases would not be considered potential DTs. Here, the limitation of the referent to one sentence is due to the fact that that sentence is functionally or thematically subordinate to the current DT. Possible modes of this functional subordination include the following:

(a) *Parenthetical statement*. Here the utterance communicates a piece of information which is in some way thematically related to the DT, and of interest to the participants, but which in no way contributes to the current informational purpose of the discourse. Consider example (30), which is taken from a larger segment which has as its DT the film *Madame Rosa*:

(30) M: [...] c'est vrai en plus, l'histoire, c'est pour ça qu'il a gagné le prix. Enfin, c'était en, euh, *Nancy*, elle aimerait beaucoup ça, c'était en, en argot, y avait énormément d'argot dedans, mais enfin, il paraît qu'c'était vrai cette histoire [...]   (II,71,6)

(Nancy is a fellow student who is particularly well-versed in French slang.)

(b) *Explanatory statement*. The given sentence may serve to explain a preceding or following DT, which usually takes the form of a proposition.

(31) M: Alors ce 'quarter', cette année, n'est-ce pas? [Laughter] Parce que à chaque fois qu'on parle entre nous du 'quarter' dernier, on dit "l'année dernière j'avais un étudiant", mais on veut dire euh
E: Parce que tu sais, *nous notre système*, c'est par année, alors quand c'est fini
M: Voilà, c'était l'année dernière!
E: C'était l'année dernière!
M: Mais j'ai dit à mes étudiants aujourd'hui, "For those of you who were with me in 1101, last year," I said, et puis ils ont ri, ils ont ri!   (I,36,14-18)

The relevant sentence is *nous notre système, c'est par année*. The current DT is something such as "M. and her French colleagues tend to use the expression *this year* instead of *this quarter*, and M's students find this amusing". Note that *notre système* is the topic only of the clause in which it occurs.

(c) *Illustration or particular case*. An example of this function is given in (32), where the higher-order discourse-topic (DT') is housing arrangements, and the current DT is roughly "There are advantages to having extra space". M's remark about their guestroom serving as a study serves as an illustration of this DT:

(32) E: [...] et aussi si t'as une grande salle à manger, tu peux l'aménager en, en, en salle d'é-, enfin en coin études ou c'que tu

veux, c'serait différent, mais si t'as un petit truc
M: Ah voilà, voilà. *Nous la chambre d'invités*, c'est la chambre, euh, où y a le bureau, la chambre de travail.
E: Oui, c'est ça, tu peux être tranquille quand tu as besoin de travailler.
M: Ah oui, ça c'est bien, hein. Ca aide énormément, ça fait une énorme différence tout d'un coup d'avoir une chambre de plus.
(I,7,7)

Notice that this case recalls Keenan and Schieffelin's (1976) use of the same terms ('particular case' and 'illustration') to describe one of the functions of LD. This is in apparent contradiction to the suggestion made here that the function of particular case or illustration is one of the ways in which a referent may be subordinated to the current DT, which would suggest the absence of LD as a general rule in such cases. Two possible solutions suggest themselves. First, it may simply be necessary to distinguish two types of cases according to the degree of importance or interest accorded to the referent in the discourse. That is, in some cases, the referent serving as an illustration may well be developed in the following discourse as a DT in its own right, while in other cases, as in (32), a single utterance may be quite sufficient to the purpose of the illustration. This explanation would be plausible, if in fact the presence of LDs in contexts such as (32) could be shown to be the exception rather than the rule, or if such cases were to be attributable to other factors, such as, for instance, the grammaticalization of LD in *c'est* ... contexts. On the other hand, if LD is frequent in contexts such as (32), where the LD-referent is not a DT, and its presence is not explainable by other factors, then one could conclude that the function of illustration or particular case favors the occurrence of LD, even where the LD-referent does not have the status of a DT. The evidence favors the first conclusion.

Though examples such as the preceding, where the LD-referent is not a DT, are less numerous than those where it is a DT, the former cases are numerous enough to pose a serious problem for the claim that LD in French has as an *essential* function the establishing or shifting of the DT. One might try to salvage this claim by substituting a notion of 'discourse entity' such as that described in the previous section for the notion of DT as defined here. That is, the notion of discourse entity could be made to include LD-referents such as those of (29)-(32) on the basis that they are in some sense important at the level of the discourse. The problem with such an approach, however, is that there no longer remains any precise content to the notion of discourse entity, discourse entities being identified by their occurrence in LDs, which is of course what we are trying to explain.

A better approach, it seems to me, is to retain the definition of DT presented here and to recognize that the association LD and DT does not hold for all instances of LD. Rather, the establishing of a new DT, as in (28) above, appears to be one of several possible LD functions. Notice that the LDs of (31) and (32) are instances of NP *c'est* ...; the near grammaticalization of this construction is argued to have pragmatic motivation in sec. 5.1.1. The LD of (30) serves to introduce a referent which is new to the discourse, a function which appears to characterize a certain number of LDs. (cf. sec. 5.2.4.)

The facts of this section are also problematic for Lambrecht's (1984b) proposal that LDs tend to occur in foregrounded and not in backgrounded discourse. (In a more recent version of his paper, Lambrecht gives much greater importance to the degree of topicality the referent has in the discourse, than to the foreground/background distinction. He notes that the difference in topicality between NP-LDs and lexical NP subjects "often correlates with the difference between foregrounded and backgrounded parts of the discourse.") Hopper and Thompson's (1980: 280) definition of background, to which Lambrecht refers, appears to correspond to my notion of subordination to the DT: "That part of a discourse which does not immediately and crucially contribute to the speaker's goal, but which merely assists, amplifies, or comments on it, is referred to as *background*. By contrast, the material which supplies the main points of the discourse is known as *foreground*." Various explanations are possible. It must be noted that Hopper and Thompson's work deals with grounding in narrative, and they point out that little is known about grounding in conversation, though they expect that the two genres are probably quite similar in this respect (282). Another factor may be the fact that the background/foreground distinction is one that leaves some room for subjective variation in its application to any particular case; no doubt related to this is the relative nature of the distinction. In fact, it is the case that examples cited here are relatively atypical; moreover, it has been suggested that these occurrences of LD may be accounted for by positing certain other LD functions distinct from that of establishing a DT. These questions will be further studied in sec. 5.2.4 below.

4. PRONOMINAL DETACHMENTS

4.1. 'Personal' pronouns: first person: *moi, nous*

One of the very basic observations concerning this corpus is that the most frequent type of left detachment is that with *moi*, the first-person singular tonic pronoun (i.e. disjunctive or nonclitic pronoun) in the lefthand position. This group accounts for 442 LDs, or 43% of the total, to which one could add 26 similar constructions with first-person plural *nous*. Moreover, these account for 69% of the LDs with pronouns as the lefthand element.

The mere prevalence of these *moi* constructions is of some interest, particularly in view of the rarity of comparable constructions in English, which appears to have more or less similar LD constructions. Of course, one explanation for the high relative frequency of the *moi* constructions, given the topic-marking function of LD, is the fact that paticipants in the speech act tend to predominate as topics of the discourse. This does not explain, however, the relative infrequency of comparable first-person constructions in English, where LDs generally appear to perform similar functions. The rarity of first- and second-person referents in English LDs is noted by Keenan and Schieffelin (1976: 246), who suggest that this is what one would expect, "if the primary function of Referent + Proposition constructions is to bring into the discourse a referent that the speaker believes is not currently in the foreground of the listener's consciousness". What is curious is that the majority of the French *moi* constructions seem to fit very well Keenan and Schieffelin's descriptions of the functions of foregrounding, namely, bringing in an alternative referent in relation to a previous predication, or a particular case of a general phenomenon under discussion, or simply giving special emphasis to a currently foregrounded referent (244-45). Thus, the difference here between French and English is apparently due to the availability, in English, of other means of accomplishing these functions, namely the use of stress and variations in intonation which are not possible with the French clitic pronouns. This observation may appear to reduce the function of pronominal LDs to the conventional notion of emphasis, the presence of the detached tonic pronoun being necessitated by the atonic character of the French clitics.

However, while the functions of LD include what are traditionally referred to as contrastive or emphatic functions, the more typical case is not strongly emphatic, as implied by these terms. Rather, the typical case of lefthand *moi* is better described in terms of topic shift (as suggested for Italian by Ochs and Duranti 1979), or, in many cases, our 'comparative' function (cf. sec. 3.3).

Lambrecht (1980) gives several syntactic arguments against the emphasis analysis of LD. That the function of lefthand *moi* is in fact much more pervasive than one of contrast or emphasis is borne out both by its mere frequency and by a significant number of occurrences in our corpus where there is nothing in the context to suggest even a weakly contrastive function. What the data suggests is that, for this variety of French, a lefthand *moi* is a quasi-obligatory marker of a shift from some other topic to the speaker as topic. Given the fact that in French, grammatical subjects are usually topical, it follows that lefthand *moi* will tend to occur whenever the immediately preceding discourse contains subjects which are non-coreferential with the speaker. This function of marking the speaker as topic explains the frequent occurrence of *moi* in turn-initial position, which has led to its description as a turn-taking device (Duranti and Ochs 1979). The following illustrate the noncontrastive use of *moi*; notice that in each case the *moi*-LD corresponds to the introduction or reintroduction of the speaker as topic:

(33) a. (The higher-level discourse-topic (DT') is the physical education part of the baccalaureat exam. C. earlier recounted her experience in the high-jump, after which M. recounted her experiences of the shotput and high-jump. C. now resumes her account.)
Alors *moi* finalement, j'suis partie, j'suis partie la première du truc. J'avais toute mon après-midi de libre. (II,34,17)

b. C: ... les Américains, bon ben, ils croient vraiment qu'ils sont gros. Y en a qui sont gros, hein.
M: Comme j'dis, c'est un problème d'obésité.
C: Oh oui.
E: Oh oui, parce que *moi*, la première fois qu'j'suis arrivée, j'ai vu des, surtout les femmes, ça des fois, c'est des monstres, hein. (II,53,8)

c. (The preceding DT is possible explanations for the apparent fact that more American women than men are overweight.)

E. Moi aussi, parce que j'trouve quand même qu'y a un pourcentage de femmes plus, plus important de, d'obèses, tu vois, vraiment d'obèses, mais

C: *Moi* en tous cas, j'ai été à un cours de claquettes mercredi, normalement c'est l'lundi mon cours de claquettes, puis j'ai deux cours à rattraper. Alors j'y vais l'mercredi. (She goes on to tell how she saw a very fat woman in special dance attire, which she thinks is a good thing.)(II,55,7-8)

Notice that, especially in (33b) and (c), the speaker-topic is introduced within the context of a higher-order DT, namely the problem of obesity in America. The turns containing the LDs serve to give a particular case illustrating or supporting the DT (b), or to illustrate a new idea (propositional DT) related to the more general DT. In both cases, the *moi*-LD signals not so much that the speaker is changing the topic to talk about herself, but rather that what follows is her contribution to the current DT. An appropriate English paraphrase would be the phrase 'as for me'. We will see the natural extension of this use of the *moi*-LD in sec. 6.2, where *moi* has no anaphor in the clause, and the clause cannot be described as constituting a comment about the speaker.

That *moi* is not simply a turn-taking device is demonstrated by its occurrence in turn-medial position as well:

(34) a. (DT = a flyer advertising French films at the University Film Society.)
C: Non, moi j'l'ai pas eu, celui-là.
M: Il me semble pas l'avoir vu, moi.
E: J'ai, j'ai, mais tu sais que dans le département, il y a, euh, il y en a, y en a plein. *Moi* j'en ai amené à peu près une vingtaine pour mes étudiants pour leur donner. (II,21,7)

b. (DT = C's apartment.)
M: Et puis il y a une partie cuisine, *moi* qui m'a émerveillée, tu vois. (I,4,15)

c. (DT = M's disappointment in not finding a serious basketball team to play with.)
C: Les trucs de groupe sans entraîneur, c'est (?)
M: Oh non non, il faut être dans une équipe qu'on connaît.
C: Que tu connais.

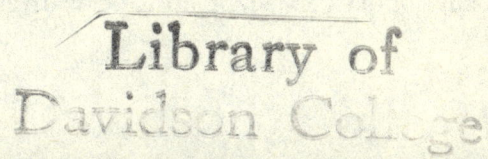

> M: Travailler dans une équipe et puis savoir c'qu'on fait.
> Moi moi ça m'intéressait en France, c'était bien, mais alors ici, voilà. (I,29,2-5)

Notice that the first person may be topical without necessarily being the grammatical subject; e.g. it may be the direct object, as in (34b) and (c), or it may be represented in a possessive determiner, as in the following:

> (35) (DT = a party E. hosted in the home where she was living)
> E: Personne était ivre, personne était ivre, mais y en avait qui avaient apporté, bon ben par exemple, une bouteille de vin blanc, tu vois euh, hein et puis certains avaient fumé et *moi*, mon intention, bien sûr, c'était de tout nettoyer. (I,75,1)

Note that where the anaphor of *moi* is not the subject, it generally bears a semantic role which may be described as highly topical, such as 'experiencer'.

Examples (34b) and (c) also illustrate again the fact that the introduction of the first-person topic does not prevent the previous topic from continuing as such; in the above cases, the previous topic retains its topicality as the grammatical subject (*qui* and *ça*) of the clause in which the first-person topic is introduced. In other words, as seen in sec. 3.6, our model of topic must allow for the coexistence of multiple topics, and the use of a LD, while usually representing a change in topic at one level, most often is consistent with the continuation of a previous topic at a higher level.

Thus, the quasi-obligatory status of lefthand *moi* as marker of a new first-person-singular topic is attributable to the pragmatic property of maximal givenness which attaches to the clitic pronouns. The rarity of such constructions in English is explained by the fact that the corresponding English pronouns are not limited to the maximal degree of givenness, but may, through various phonological modulations, refer to an individual which is a new discourse-topic. That is, I see the French *moi* constructions as corresponding to English *I* (or *me* or *my*) with what I would call moderate stress (i.e. *Í used to do it* vs. unstressed *I úsed to do it* vs. emphatically stressed *Í used to do it.*) There remains the fact that English uses LD rather than stress and intonation, i.e. more 'radical' means, to introduce new NPs. This difference in the treatment of pronouns and NPs may be explained by Keenan and Schieffelin's hypothesis, i.e. that the speaker and hearer require less drastic means of introduction because they are so immediate to the speech situation. In the same way, the immediacy of the speech act participants probably accounts for the tendency of *moi* to be relatively unstressed, while NP detachments usually carry moderate stress (cf. 3.2 above).[17]

Some further remarks are in order, concerning the description of the *moi*-LD as a marker of a new first-person topic. The corpus includes some examples which are problematic for the proposed generalization; either there appears to be a shift to the speaker as topic without the use of a *moi*-LD, or a *moi*-LD does not correspond to the promotion of the speaker to topic status. We will look at some of these cases now.

It must first be noted that the *moi*-LD marks the speaker as a topic of the *discourse*, and not simply a sentence-topic (cf. sec. 3.6 for discussion of this distinction). In other words, the occurrence of the *moi* LD is not automatic in every case in which a first-person subject follows other disreferent subjects. Consider the following:

(36) E: Vous savez qu'y a des massages, c'est aussi organisé par l'Université, tu dois apporter ton partenaire. J'ai vu ça, tu sais, 'Mini-course'. Alors euh, la dernière fois, j'étais en train d'feuilleter, tu sais, un p'tit peu c'qui s'passait et y avait, et alors j'ai, y a des massages et ils demandent, pas d'prob-[laughter], que tu amènes avec toi ton partenaire.
Alors là, j'ai vraiment
C: C'est "Bring your own bottle".
E: Vraiment, je m'suis dit, mais qu'est-ce que c'est? (II,6,17)

One might have expected a *moi*-LD accompanying the introduction of the speaker in *j'ai vu ça*, and such an occurrence would in fact be possible and not unnatural. This context appears to be similar to those of (33b) and (c) and (34a-c) above. However, I would argue that (36) differs in significant ways from the contexts of both (33) and (34). First, (36) differs from (33) in that here the speaker already has the floor (at the point of the first occurrence of the first-person pronoun), which is not the case in (33). In other words, no turn-taking device is necessary. This is true also for the contexts of (34), but in (34), the speaker can be said to have a certain importance as a DT in her own right. I think that the *moi*-LDs of (34) may also be said to be mildly emphatic. Returning to (36), this context is clearly incompatible with any emphasis on the first-person subject. Moreover, here the speaker bears relatively little importance as a topic in its own right, but is instead subordinated to the current DT. The previous DT is massage parlors, and the purpose of E's turn is to relate information about a certain class in massage and her surprise at the description of the activity.

(37) is another example of the absence of a *moi*-LD where the speaker-referent is not already a topic:

(37) M: Et dites-moi, comment se fait-il que ici, aux Etats-Unis, pour les choses en argent, c'est très rare de trouver le poinçon?
E: Ah bon? Tu sais que le poinçon
M: Oui oui, j'ai souvent (été) à Dayton's pour les wedding lists là, mais je ne trouve pas le poinçon. (III,11,16)

As in (36), though the first-person referent is 'new' at this point of the discourse, it does not attain the status of a topic of the discourse. The DT is *le poinçon*, or the question, why is the *poinçon* ('silver stamp') rare in the United States, and the function of the proposition containing the first-person referent is simply evidence supporting the presupposition contained in the DT. Thus, the speaker does not qualify as a DT. Thus, the description of clitic pronouns without accompanying detachments as being limited to contexts of maximal givenness requires some qualification. The clitic may be used alone even when its referent is new to the discourse, but only if the speaker does not wish to give that referent the status of a topic of the discourse. We will see below (sec. 5.2.5) that this same principle operates with respect to the distinction between lexical NP subjects and lexical NP detachments. That is, lexical NP subjects, like nondetached first-person subject clitics whose referents are 'new' to the discourse, tend to be nontopical and occur in backgrounded parts of the discourse.

Most of the cases of nonoccurrence of *moi* where it would be expected (i.e. where the speaker is 'new' to the discourse) are of the preceding type. There are a few other cases, however, where the speaker clearly is a DT. I think that these cases, which are restricted to only one of the speakers, are explainable by stylistic factors. Consider the following:

(38) (previous DT = costs of various foods and eating habits of the participants while in America)

B: Il vous faut encore du jus d'orange? Y en a encore.
M: Non merci.
B: Tu en prends?
E: Oui, j'vais en prendre un p'tit peu.
C: J'essaie d'étaler mais c'est sans succès hein.
E: Merci.
C: Bon, ça fait rien.

> M: Non merci, vraiment. Vous savez, Madame Barnes, je bois très peu, très peu. Il y a plusieurs jours, ça m'arrive très souvent où, du moment où je me lève au moment où je me couche, où je n'ai même pas bu un verre d'eau entier. (I,27,10)

One would expect a *moi*-LD accompanying M's *je bois très peu*, since the speaker-referent is new, and it also is a DT. I believe the absence of a *moi*-LD can be attributed to the fact that M. adopts here a more formal style in order to address me, as indicated by the use of *vous savez* rather than *tu sais* (which is often used by other speakers, as well as by M, with no specific addressee).[18]

To summarize then, the traditional notions of contrast and emphasis associated with lefthand pronouns have been given, in the case of *moi* in particular, a more precise content (which has, moreover, a more general application), in terms of the introduction of the speaker as a discourse-topic. It is in fact the case that a large proportion of these cases may also be characterized as comparative, in the sense described in section 3.3. For example:

> (39) a. (C. has been recounting her childhood days at summer camp, in particular, how being unathletic she disliked hikes and certain group games.)
> M: *Moi* j'adorais tout ce qui était jeux. Dès qu'ça bougeait, dès qu'on était pas assis. J'pouvais pas rester assise sur une chaise. Le résultat, regardez! Deux ou trois heures comme ça. Dès qu'j'suis assise sur une chaise, je supporte pas. Là je bouge toujours mes pieds.
> C: Oui, regarde! *Moi* c'est le contraire.
> E: Oui, *moi* non plus, j'ai pas c'problème. (II,30,6-8)
>
> b. (In the previous discourse, M. recounts how, contrary to her expectations, she did very well on the history-geography portion of the baccalauréat exam, then E. briefly reports that this was her best grade, since it was her favorite subject.)
> C: *Moi* par contre, tu sais, y avait l'anglais en, en écrit. J'me disais, l'anglais, c'est c'qui va m'sauver, j'vais avoir au moins quinze. Paf! Douze! J'me disais merde! Oh et puis en fin de compte, j'l'ai eu quand même. (II,41,1-3)

There remain a few cases, however, to which neither of the functions of topic shift nor comparison are applicable. In these cases, the only applicable description is that of ordinary emphasis in the conventional sense (i.e. not in the sense of Lambrecht's emphatic function). For example:

(40) (previous DT = silly answers their students have given to certain questions on tests)
E: C'est comme pour Balzac, tu vois, la rue Balzac, alors euh, j'leur dis euh, ah Balzac! Qui c'est Balzac? Alors euh, y en a quand même tu vois, y en avait deux qui savaient que c'était un écrivain.
M: Ah voilà! Moi j'avais
E: Un écrivain français du dix-neuvième. Ah ils m'ont dit du dix-septième, j'ai dit non, mais du dix-neuvième. Ben i'savaient que c'était un écrivain.
C: C'est pas mal ça déjà, hein.
E: Puis alors *moi* j'leur dis toujours que en France y a pas de, de, de, de numéro pour les rues euh (I,51,10-14)

The *moi* of E's last turn is not a case of topic shift, since E and her students are already topical; neither is it explicitly comparative. It may be described as adding a slight emphasis, which I would paraphrase as "I don't know about *you*, but as for me ...". In other words, this kind of emphasis actually involves a sort of implicit comparison with whatever other referents are appropriate, according to the context. (It is this interpretation, for instance, that characterizes the frequent occurrences of *moi* with *je trouve*, *je dis*, and similar expressions which serve to emhasize the speaker's belief in some proposition.)

Finally, there are certain cases of *moi*-LD which represent a significant extension of the usual topic-comment relation. The syntactic correlate of this extension is the absence of an anaphor in the accompanying clause. Although this phenomenon is most marked with respect to *moi*, these cases will be studied in section 6.2 with other cases of 'no anaphor' LDs. It should be noted that such constructions are in no way exceptional with respect to the functions enumerated here, i.e. they are all describable in terms of turn taking, topic shift, comparison, or emphasis.

The first-person plural pronoun *nous* occurs in 36 LDs in this corpus, either with no anaphor in the clause (10 tokens) or with the subject clitic *on* (which replaces standard French *nous* in this dialect). The functions of these LDs are comparable to those of *moi*-LDs. Though most instances are describable as comparative, in a few cases only the topic shift description applies, e.g.:

(41) a. (DT = teaching of culture in the beginning French course)

Oh oui, ça, tu vois, c'est après justement, il faut équilibrer, après un cours avec de la grammaire, on est (?), euh, oui, c'est ça, que ce soit enfin, mais par example, *nous* on fait les directions demain, alors j'ai amené des, des cartes postales sur Paris, tu vois ... (I,50,13)

b. (At the end of the recording session, participants are discussing arrangements for getting home; B. has another meeting to go to.)

C: Mais à quelle heure vous devez être là-bas?

B: Mais, ça n'fait rien, j'y serai un peu, un petit peu en retard, mais

C: Ben oui mais euh, *nous*, on aurait pu euh (I,70,8)

4.2. 'Nonpersonal' pronouns: *ça*

The other frequent type of Pro-detachment is that with demonstrative *ça*. Of the total of 139 tokens, 115 are with the verb *être*. Lambrecht (1981: 6) claims that in nonstandard French, *ça* replaces both *cela* and *ce* of the standard language. Only the first of these replacements is evident in this corpus, as we find the standard *ce sera* rather than *ça sera* as predicted by Lambrecht. According to Lambrecht, it is only before the present and possibly imperfect forms of *être* that *ce* (i.e. *c-*) remains. What is not evident from this description is the fact that standard *cela est* or *cela était* is regularly replaced in the nonstandard language by a left-detached *ça*, e.g.: *ça c'est bien*, *ça c'était bien*. In other words, *ça c-*... represents a deictic subject pronoun, while *c-*... represents a merely anaphoric subject (before *est/était*).

It is precisely this difference between deictic and anaphoric function that is traditionally described as emphasis. Note that, in contrast to the personal pronouns, we would not expect *ça* to have topic shift as a major function, especially with a comparative connotation. Nevertheless, the function of *ça c-* is related to that of *moi je* in that *c-* shares with *je* the property of being largely restricted to contexts where the referent is maximally given or topical. While the alternation between *c'est* and *ça c'est* is not quite as systematic as that between *je* and *moi je*, there are still some discernible patterns with respect to typical environments. In the case of *c'est*, the fact that *c-* is essentially an empty place-holder (cf. sec. 5.1.1) means that its reference must be obvious from the context because of its immediacy and/or its status as topic of the discourse. Thus, one might say that the prototypic occurrence of *c-* is that where its antecedent is most immediate, i.e. with a left-detached NP, e.g. *Ed c'est un musicien*. *Ca c-*, on the other hand, as a deictic, finds its reference by pointing to something which is salient in either the situational or the preceding linguistic context; its referent/antecedent is typically not as immediate as that of *c-*. I will try to demonstrate this difference, as well as other properties of *ça c-* in what follows.

Where *ça c-* takes its reference from the linguistic context, it is typically used to make an evaluative comment on a situation described in the preceding turn or series of utterances. Moreover, just as one points to an object only in initiating conversation about it, lefthand *ça* typically occurs with a speaker's first reference to the entity/situation, and is not usually repeated in successive references to it (and is thus similar to lefthand *moi*). The following example is representative:

(42) (M. has been telling how she worked for five months as a waitress in a Middle Eastern restaurant.)
M: [...] L'année dernière, le 1er de l'An, j'ai travaillé quatorze heures d'affilé, sans une minute de pause, pas une seule minute de pause,
E: C'est vrai?
M: et j'ai fait moins de quinze dollars. Parce qu'il avait 'the special deal, thirthy dollars a person', mais il n'avait dit à personne que le tip n'était pas inclus. Oui, ça c'était affreux. Je n'oublierai pas ce 1er de l'An. Cette année, autant t'dire, au 1er de l'An, j'étais à la maison, j'travaillais pas. Ca m'a servi. C'était affreux, affreux! (III,41,1-3)

Notice that the referent of *ça* is the event which is recounted in the immediately preceding discourse. *Ca* represents the first explicit reference to the event as a whole, so in this sense it establishes the event as the current topic of the discourse. Note also the later reference to the same event with *c-* alone.

I do not mean to argue, of course, that the use of *ça c-* is obligatory in a context such as the above. In most cases, either *ça c-* or *c-* would be acceptable. The emphatic effect that results from the use of *ça c-* in such contexts may be seen as the result of pointing to the referent when no such pointing is necessary. There are some cases, however, where the substitution of *c-* for *ça c-* leads to unclear or unsuccessful reference; I believe these cases provide evidence for the foregoing description of the difference between *c-* and *ça c-*. Consider for example (43), which follows a rather extended discussion of the various dishes that M. teaches in her cooking class:

(43) Alors *ça* c'est mon menu international. (I,38,7)

The immediately preceding DT is the weight-consciousness of Americans in the summer. Here the use of *ça c-* is occasioned by the need to point back to a referent, or actually a series of referents, which are less immediate and which are spread over a stretch of discourse.

Similarly, *ça c-* may serve to single out one of several possible referents, as in the following:

(44) (DT = a particular delicatessen store)
Ils ont plusieurs sortes de jambon, alors ils ont l'jambon ordinaire, l'aut'jambon tu sais, en boîte là qui euh, dégouline d'eau et pis t'as l'vrai jambon, alors *ça* c'est excellent et c'est pas vraiment très cher parce que l'autre fois on avait (I,44,22)

When an utterance with *ça c-* is preceded by one or more instances of *c'est* ..., it sometimes is the case that the referent of *ça c-* is related to that of the preceding *c-* but has a broader scope. For example:

(45) (DT = the difficulty of teaching the second-quarter French course)
M: C'est du monologue pratiquement, 1102! C'est
E: *Ca* c'est ennuyeux!
M: Ah là là!
E: C'est vraiment ennuyeux! Quand c'est un monologue et que toi tu, tu expliques la grammaire et c'est tout, alors là!
(III,37,13-16)

The referent of the preceding *c-* is the course 1102, whereas the referent of *ça c-* is the reduction of the course to a monologue on grammar. This broadening of the referent, or at least the nonidentity of the two referents, follows naturally from the preceding observation that *ça c-* is generally restricted to initial references to a topic.

The relation between *ça c-*... and *c-*... has an apparent parallel, before verbs other than *être*, in the pair *ça ça* V ... and *ça* V ....[19] Occurrences of *ça ça* V ... are of course much less frequent, due simply to the predominance of the verb *être*. However, the seven cases of *ça ça* V ... in the corpus are clearly comparative or emphatic and are consistently marked by a high pitch rise on the LD. In contrast, the *ça c'est* LD may be similarly marked, but often is relatively unmarked. This suggests that in fact, the pair *ça ça* V .../*ça* V ... is not, with respect to pragmatic function, strictly parallel to the pair *ça c'est*/*c'est*. A possible explanation is that, in spite of its phonological/syntactic status of clitic, *ça* in *ça* V ... differs from *c-* in being less restricted to referents of maximal givenness or immediacy.

5. LEXICAL NP-DETACHMENTS

About one-half of all NP-detachments are of the type NP *c'est* ...[20] The corpus contains 198 tokens of this type, with the remaining subject-anaphor constructions being comprised of 29 with the anaphor *ça* and 81 with one of what I call the personal subject clitics *il(s)/elle(s)*.

5.1. With nonpersonal anaphor
5.1.1. NP *c'est* ...

The data of this corpus strongly suggest that the use of LD with lexical subjects of *être* is quasi-obligatory where *ce* (*c-*) is an appropriate anaphor. Inspection of the cases of lexical subjects of *être* without LD reveals that the majority of these are in contexts where *ce* is not an appropriate anaphor. That is, for the most part, the subject is an animate noun, and the constituent following *être* is an Adjective Phrase (AP), e.g. *ma mère est catholique*. Another clear case where *ce* would be an inappropriate anaphor is the case of an inanimate plural NP which does not allow (in the given context) the sort of collective interpretation necessary to allow the use of *c'est*. For example:

(46) (describing a particular manner of holding a cup)
    a. tous les doigts sont en-d'sous
    b. #tous les doigts, c'est en d'sous

This is in contrast to the case of singular inanimates, where colloquial French, as is well-known, commonly allows the replacement, even before *être* + AP, of standard *il/elle* by *ce*. While I would argue that most instances of this replacement may be correlated with certain semantic properties, there are some cases which do not appear to be amenable to this kind of explanation. Thus, generally speaking, both *ce* and *il/elle* must be considered appropriate anaphors of singular inanimates, regardless of the nature of the constituent following *être*. The consequence of taking this fact into account is a slight increase in the number of exceptions to the abovementioned generalization that nondetached lexical NP subjects of *être* have *il/elle* and not *ce* as an appropriate anaphor.

There are as well a few exceptions to the foregoing generalization where *ce* would be an entirely appropriate anaphor, even in the standard language. In some of these cases, it appears that the nonoccurrence of LD is attributable to the nontopical status of the NP. For example, the following is an excerpt from an extended discussion of the *poinçon*, the official stamp found on objects of precious metals, and why M. has not found such a stamp in America:

> (47) E: [...] Donc, ton poinçon te donne le pourcentage d'or. Alors il varie selon les pays. La France
> M: Oui mais ici, l'problème, c'est qu'j'en ai pas vu.
> E: Oui *la France* est un des pays qui a le plus fort, le plus fort poinçon, aussi bien pour l'argent que pour l'or. Donc, bien sûr, c'est cher quand t'achètes de l'or ou d'l'argent en France, mais c'est parce que c'est l'plus pur.   (II,11,17-19)

A plausible explanation for the absence of *c'* following *la France* at the beginning of E's last turn is that *la France* is not, and does not become, a topic of the discourse, but rather is subordinated to the current DT, *le poinçon*. (Cf. sec. 5.2.4 for discussion of this constraint.) This approach would also suggest that LD would not be expected in nonasserted embedded clauses, as in the relative clause of the following example:

> (48) j'ai été élevée dans une culture où *un jour sans viande* est un jour atroce, misérable.   (I,32,22)

However, neither the property of representing a discourse-topic nor the context of asserted clause can be construed as necessary conditions for LD, since counterexamples to both are found in the corpus (cf. (24) and (30)-(32) above). That such 'counterexamples' involving NP *c'est* ... are frequent, in fact considerably more frequent than examples such as (47) and (48), where LD does not occur though *c-* is an appropriate anaphor, corroborate what is suggested by the preceding observations concerning the frequency of NP *c'est*... , namely that this structure is in the process of becoming grammaticalized.

In fact, the LD construction with *c'est* is grammaticalized in the standard written language in certain contexts. Grevisse (1969: 465) states that the construction is obligatory in the following contexts:

> (a) when the attribute (i.e. predicate complement) is a personal pronoun: *Mon meilleur auxiliaire, c'est vous.*

(b) when, after a singular subject, the attribute is plural: *Le gibier du lion, ce ne sont pas moineaux*.

In the following contexts, the construction is described as almost obligatory:

(a) when the attribute is a clause introduced by *que*: *Une chose regrettable, c'est qu'il a manqué de politesse*.
(b) when the sentence begins with *ce* + relative: *Ce que je sais le mieux, c'est mon commencement*.
(c) when the attribute is an infinitive: *L'héroïsme du pauvre, c'est d'immoler l'envie*.

Of the 198 tokens of the NP *c'est* type, 36 occur in one of the contexts (a)-(c), and four more are similar to (a) but have the clause introduced by *quand* or *parce que*. As one might expect, the spoken language represented here differs from the standard written language described by Grevisse in that all of the above contexts are obligatory contexts for LD, as there are no such contexts without LD.

Thus, the nearly obligatory use of the NP *c'est* LD in the spoken language might be seen as an extension of the same construction's use in the standard written language. This suggests the hypothesis that the construction is similar in pragmatic function in both kinds of contexts, i.e., those described in the preceding paragraph, and those which do not show any of the preceding properties. I shall argue that this hypothesis is correct, and that the high frequency of LD with *c'est* is related to the semantics of *c'est*, together with the most basic pragmatic function of LD.

It is interesting that Lambrecht (1984b: 26) states that lexical subject NPs (i.e. without LD) in spoken French "occur in their vast majority in *intransitive* clauses, in particular in clauses containing the verb *être* 'to be'". This statement appears to be contrary to the evidence of the present corpus. In fact, in this corpus, of the 165 instances of subject NPs without LD (where LD would have been possible), only about 30% are with the verb *être*. Clearly, *être* figures in a much larger percentage of the instances of NP-LDs (198 out of 389, or more than 50%). Since, as pointed out above, LD is associated with *être* and the anaphor *ce*, what is crucial to an understanding of these LDs is the semantic distinction that opposes *ce* and the alternative 'personal' anaphors *il(s)/elle(s)* in combination with *être*. Very simply, this fairly well-known distinction may be described in terms of an identificational vs. a predicational use of *être*. This distinction is clearly seen in the following false start and reformulation:

(49) *Les biscuits à la cuiller*, tu sais, c'est des, ils sont longs comme ça à peu près (III,50,17)

The speaker first sets out to give a definition of the pastry in question, as indicated by *c'est des*, but then changes to a description, switching to *ils sont*.

In order to answer the question of why LD should be associated with the identificational and not with the predicational use of *être*, let us look again at the contexts for NP *c'est* LDs in the standard written language. What do all of these have in common? The last three, the 'almost obligatory' contexts, share a certain syntactic complexity in that each has an embedded clause, or infinitive, in either subject or predicate complement position. This seems to suggest an explanation in terms of difficulty of perceptual processing. However, there is no comparable syntactic complexity in the two obligatory contexts. Nevertheless, one might say, for these cases, that the LD serves to 'mediate' the relation between the subject and the predicate complement, in that these two, in each case, form a rather unexpected combination, either because the complement is a pronoun which is somewhat unusual in this position, or because of a lack of number agreement. I think this suggests a more general explanation which may account for the extension of the NP *c'est* detachment in spoken French. The 'mediation' between the subject and the predicate complement which is achieved by LD is accomplished by means of breaking up the unitary proposition into two clearly articulated utterance parts. This articulation of the utterance into two components is of course the most basic of the pragmatic functions of LD. Returning to the two different uses of *être*, while a predicational statement predicates some quality of a given term, an identificational statement presents two terms in a relation of identity. Inasmuch as an identificational statement is essentially a two-term equation, the LD construction is particularly well-suited to this kind of statement since it sets off clearly the two terms of the equation. In other words, LD is a sort of iconic representation of the identity relation denoted by *c'est*. Being semantically empty, the pronoun *ce* is ideally suited to fill the obligatory pronoun slot.

Given the possible replacement in colloquial French of *il/elle* by *ce* mentioned above, there are of course some instances of NP *c'est* ... which correspond to the predicational rather than to the identificational use. Even so, there are certain semantic properties which characterize most cases of NP *c'est* + AP and distinguish these from what I would call a strict predicational use of *être*. Though this topic cannot be treated here in detail, I think a few comments are in order. Larsson (1979: 138-39), comparing the following two utterances:

(50) a. La soupe à l'oignon, c'est bon.
    b. La soupe à l'oignon est bonne.

claims that the reference of the detached NP in (50a) is necessarily generic while the subject NP of (50b) has a very strong tendency to be interpreted as specific. While it is true that the large majority of the cases of NP *c'est* + AP are with NPs of generic interpretation, the alternation is not quite so categorical as suggested by Larsson. (This is in accord with what one would expect, given that the generic/specific distinction is usually derived from the linguistic context of the NP.) On the one hand, the corpus includes examples of the nondetached structure of (50b) with generic reference, e.g. *la viande est excellente; la viande est bien meilleure ici.* There is also one instance of LD with a personal subject clitic where the NP is clearly generic in interpretation:

(51) Mais *la viande*, elle est pas chère en général ici.
(I,25,12)

On the other hand, there are a significant number of counterexamples to the association of NP *c'est* with genericness; careful examination of these suggests that another more general principle is at work.

Consider the following:

(52) a. *la table sur laquelle on mange*, *c*'est dans la salle à manger
(I,4,15)
   b. *Tours*, *c*'est connu. (III,17,9)
   c. Non non non, celui, *celui d'la piscine*, non, *c*'est pas si sophistiqué. (*celui = le sauna*) (II,5,1)
   d. (M. is describing how her students stared at her heavy winter boots when she entered the classroom with them on.)
      La tête des étudiants, *c*'est comme ça! (II,14,12)
   e. "*Garde à Vue*", *c*'est pas cette semaine. (II,19,3)
   f. (after being offered orange juice by the hostess)
      Oui, *un jus d'orange*, *c*'est très bien, oui. (II,2.10)

The detached NP in all of the above can only be interpreted as specific, i.e. nongeneric. In (a), the detached NP includes a relative clause; my impression, on inspection of the data, is that the tendency in written French to use LD where the subject NP is a *ce que* or *ce qui* relative is generalized in the spoken language to any type of relative clause. Examples (b)-(f) are more indicative of the general principle that I think is most often involved. The use of *c'est* with the city name *Tours* in (b) is explainable by recourse to conventional notions concerning the use of *ce* with antecedents having no grammatical gender, but also note that the referent is of course a place. Similarly, the use of *c-* referring to the swimming pool's sauna in (c) may be due to the fact that the sauna is conceived of more as a place than as an entity. In (d), the replacement of *c'* by *elle* would seem to suggest one individual head, when in fact it must of course refer collectively to the heads of all the students, which is precisely the kind of reference allowed by *ce*. In (e), *cette semaine* is of course an Adverb Phrase, rather than an Adjective Phrase, which tells when the given film is playing, rather than describing the film itself. Finally, in (f), it is again not a quality of the NP *jus d'orange* that is expressed by the complement *très bien*; rather, the speaker is expressing the fact that a glass of orange juice is a choice that fits her taste at the moment. The general principle, then, is that *il(s)/elle(s)* refer to the thing as an individual entity (or a plurality of individual entities), and the complement following *il/elle est* expresses a quality adhering in the thing itself. That neither of these restrictions holds for *c'est* is in complete accord with the preceding discussion of *c'est* as the marker of the identification function; that is, *c'est* is simply a relator of two terms or expressions, which carries no semantic content other than the bringing into relation of the two expressions. This difference between *c'est* and *il/elle est* can be seen as well in some of the generic uses of *c'est*; for example:

(53) Moi j'trouve qu'*une maison*, c'est vraiment important. (I,61,22)

Here the speaker is not attributing importance to a house itself, but rather to the condition of owning or living in a house. The following:

(54) *Les choux à la crème*, c'est bien.   (I.46,13)

is like (52f) above in that the speaker is actually approving the choice of cream puffs as a recipe to be made with a group of students during an evening party, rather than saying anything about cream puffs themselves.

Thus, given the reduced semantic content of *c'est*, the referential properties of *ce/c'* are best described by way of negation of the restrictions on *il(s)/elle(s)*. Not being limited to distinct individual entities as referents, *ce/c-* is open to virtually any sort of referent. While generics might be considered the nonindividual referent type par excellence, they are in fact only one of various possible realizations of the referential possibilities of *c'est*.[21]

In the spoken language, *c'est* has become grammatically as well as semantically neutral; that is, it is not restricted to singular number agreement.[22] The use of LD cited by Grevisse where a singular subject occurs with a plural predicate complement finds its extension in the spoken language where *c'est* occurs quite commonly following an LD-expression of plural number, e.g.:

(55) a. Oh mais *les substituts*, c'est horrible. (I,37,17)
 b. *Les résurrections*, c'est rare, quand même. (III,70,16)
 c. Mais j'crois qu'*les couleurs de Noël, rouge et vert*, c'est beaucoup plus important ici qu'en France. (I,18,19)

In each case, there are of course semantic factors which facilitate the 'neutralization' of the number feature; that is, in general, the plural NP in fact refers to a unitary or a collective entity, as in the case of plural generics, to cite the most frequent case. Moreover, *c'est* may link NPs in every possible combination of grammatical numbers. For example:

(56) (Plural subject, singular complement)
 a. *Cent quatre-vingt-cinq dollars*, c'est rien. (I,4,21)
 b. *les adjectifs démonstratifs*, c'est pas un point d'grammaire difficile (III,32,1)
(57) (Singular subject, plural complement)
 M: [...] en principe, en hiver, c'qui marche très bien (donc), c'est le fameux couscous et l'étagine, l'étagine tunisien.
 C: C'est quoi?
 M: *Etagine*, c'est des genres de ragoûts (I,39,4)
(58) (Plural subject, plural complement)
 B: Enfin y a des baptistes et des baptistes.
 E: Oh ben *ceux-là*, c'est des purs, hein. (*ceux-là* refers to a particular Baptist family) (I,77,13)

C'est has been described as a semantically and grammatically neutral marker of the relation of identity. However, even this description is still a bit too restrictive to cover all the uses of *c'est* in the spoken language, since in some cases the relation between the two related expressions is not one of strict identity. The actual precise relation between the two expressions is of course inferrable from the context and from extralinguistic knowledge. Thus, the absence of semantic or grammatical restrictions on *c'est* makes of it a general linking device, which is extremely useful in unplanned spoken discourse, since it reduces the amount of necessary planning and allows the speaker to be less explicit than would be appropriate in planned-discourse settings. For example:

(59) (recounting an incident in a restaurant where she was a waitress)
Alors euh, y a, y a quand même deux tables qui m'ont laissé cinq dollars sur la table, *une des tables*, c'était le copain de mon mari (III,41,14)

(60) C: Ca c'est marrant. J'ai jamais rien eu, moi, j'ai, décidément, j'ai rien d'intéressant à raconter. Alors rien!
M: Mais si! *Ta mère au syndicat*, c'était pas mal. (III,80,16)

(61) E: (recounting a trip to New York where she stayed with a friend)
Moi ça m'est pas revenu vraiment, enfin bon, bien sûr, y a l'voyage, mais enfin, ça c'est pas vraiment cher.
M: Ah oui! *Le voyage*, c'est normal. (II,78,4)

Notice that the antecedents of *c'* in (60) and (61) are actually interpreted as 'l'histoire de ta mère au syndicat' and 'le fait que tu paies le voyage,' respectively. These cases of 'sloppy identity' find a further extension in the kind of utterances studied in 6.2 below, where *ce/c'* cannot be described as the anaphor of the left-detached expression.

Thus, we have proposed two different types of motivation for NP *c'est* LDs, which may of course apply simultaneously. The first type, applicable in particular to cases where the predicate complement bears a relation of identity with the LD-expression, sees the LD structure as an iconic representation of the identity relation. In order to account for cases where the relation of the predicate complement is rather one of predication (i.e. the complement is adjectival), a second type of motivation, more specifically semantic in nature, has been cited. This second motivation involves the exploitation of certain referential properties of *c-* as opposed to *il(s)/elle(s)*. That these two types of motivation are in fact closely related is attested by the fact that it is precisely the semantic 'neutrality' or unmarkednes of *ce* which makes possible the conversational use of *c'est* as a sort of 'all-purpose' pragmatic connector.

While the identificational relation in particular may be seen as a sort of topic-comment relation par excellence, it should be remembered that neither of the two motivations described requires that the LD-referent be a topic of the discourse. Accordingly, many of the LD-referents of the preceding examples do not enjoy the status of DTs (many are restricted to the clause in which they occur).

It should be noted that there is another group of NP *c'est* LDs which do not either qualify as DTs, but for slightly different reasons. This rather special group of NP *c'est* LDs are the cleft constructions described by Grevisse's second and third 'nearly obligatory' contexts, i.e. sentences beginning with *ce qu-* relatives, or where the predicate complement is an infinitive or a clause introduced by *que*. The following illustrate two of the most frequent LD-expressions of this type:

(62) a. *c'qu'y a*, c'est qu'i'faut que j'me renseigne un p'tit peu pour les, les, j't'ai dit, si j'ai droit, enfin j'ai certainement droit à une couverture aussi bien pour euh, médicale que, même si j'veux faire un sport quelconque, mais i'faut que j'me renseigne, je sais pas, je sais pas, je sais pas où c'est. (III,28,17)
b. *le problème*, c'est que quand tu les mets en groupe, ça prend tellement d'temps. (III,37,18)

In sec. 5.2.2, I refer to these types of LD-expressions as Non Discourse Referents, since they do not constitute discourse referents in the sense of Karttunen (1976). The syntactic evidence for this description is the fact that, with this type of LD, the 'givenness' of the LD-expression does not extend beyond the initial anaphor in the immediately following clause. These sorts of expressions are never referred to again in the following discourse because they do not refer to discourse referents, but rather are simply devices for introducing and relating to the current discourse some other discourse entity, which most often is a proposition. (Notice in (62) that although the following discourse contains an anaphor which theoretically could refer back to the LD expression (*c'* and *ça* respectively), in neither instance is this the case.) We will not consider these cleft structures in detail, but will simply note that these may be considered a kind of conversational device which, like identificational *c'est* in general, makes use of the articulated structure of LD. Prince (1978) claims that *wh*-clefts are given, in the sense that they represent inferences which are situationally appropriate (presumably NPs such as *le problème* are similar in this respect). Notice then that the use of the cleft construction assures the preferred pattern of 'old information' (what is presupposed) coming first, followed by 'new information'. This is particularly evident in cases where the complement following *c'est* is an ordinary NP rather than a clause:

(63) en principe, en hiver, *c'qui marche très bien* (donc), c'est le fameux couscous et l'étagine (I,38,18)

Where the complement is a clause, the LD-expression which introduces it also functions much like a sentential adverb in indicating the speaker's attitude concerning the proposition. The quasi-autonomous nature of these LD-expressions is apparent in the following example where the connecting *c'est que* is omitted:[23]

(64) Et puis *c'qu'y a*, bon ben, André euh, c'est un musicien. (I,7,12)

5.1.2. NP *ça* V

The view that *ça* in NP *ça* V ... is a morphological variant of the clitic *ce* that occurs before verbs other than *être* is borne out by analysis of the instances of this construction in the corpus. Though the frequency of this construction is of course much lower than that of the NP *c'est* construction due to the much greater versatility of the verb *être* (and particularly of *c'est*, given its reduced semantic and grammatical content, as observed above), the referential properties of *ça*, and its relation to the preceding NP, are very similar to what was observed for certain cases of *ce*. The antecedent is generally either a genderless NP, (i.e. a headless relative (*ce que* ...), a word or phrase in citation (*mais "les restes de fromages", ça veut dire quoi?*), an infinitive, or a foreign word) or a generic NP:

(65) a. *La clarinette*, c'est, ça a une pureté de son. (I,60,11)
b. *les dents d'sagesse*, ça pousse ou ça pousse pas (III,9,17)

There are a few cases similar to the examples of 'sloppy identity' referred to above where the actual NP antecedent is an NP with gender, but the intended referent is something other than the referent of that NP, e.g.:

(66) (E. is recounting a visit by a Belgian to her French class.)
E: Bon, personne savait où était la Belgique, alors j'ai fait vite un, des(-), un dessin et puis j'ai dit: c'est là!
.....
E: Non mais, euh, oui, *la Belgique*, ça avait pas beaucoup marché. (I,52,11)

Finally, there are several cases where the NP antecedent is grammatically plural but is interpretable in the context as semantically singular, e.g.:

(67) a. Le mois de février est court, alors, ça nous, *quatre jours*, ça joue, hein quand même. (III,23,12)
b. Non puisque *les poux*, c'est, c'est, ça reste dans le, dans la chaleur des cheveux. (III,61,2)
c. *Les oeufs, les poulets, tout ça*, ça va tellement être mélangé. (I,34,19)

In summary, then, NP *ça* V ... shares with NP *c'est* ... the second type of motivation described above, since *ça* shares the semantic properties of *ce*.

Of course, NP *ça* V ... does not share the first type of motivation, the iconic representation of the identity relation. That it is in fact this iconic motivation which accounts for the grammaticalization or nearly obligatory status of NP *c'est* ... is supported by the fact that NP *ça* V ... does not have the same extension as NP *c'est*. This difference is reflected in various ways in the data. First, where NP *ça* V ... occurs, it generally is the case that either the referent is a DT, or there are clear semantic reasons for the use of *ça*. We saw above that this is not the case for NP *c'est* ..., where a number of instances have referents which are not DTs, and there is no clear semantic motivation for the use of *c-*. Secondly, if we look at cases of nondetached lexical NP subjects which could have *ça* as a possible anaphor, there are proportionately more of these than there are of nondetached lexical NP subjects having *ce* as a possible anaphor. That is, if NP *ça* V ... were comparable to NP *c'est* in its extension, we would expect to find relatively fewer cases of nondetachment such as the following, regardless of whether or not the referent is topical in the discourse, or generic or specific in reference:

(68) a. La machine à laver ne marche pas. (I,5,5)
 b. Le fruit auquel je pensais fond sous la langue. (I,17,7)
 c. J'te dis, j'voulais jouer au tennis, alors euh, la balle venait de tous les coins [...] (I,30,11)

5.2. With personal anaphor: NP *il/elle* ...

We have so far examined pronominal detachments and lexical NP-detachments with the anaphor *ce/ça*. In the case of the former, there were found to be very clear pragmatic factors governing their occurrence; in the case of the latter, for *ce* in particular, the LD construction was shown to be nearly obligatory, and the grammaticalization of this construction was related to the semantics of *c'est* and the basic function of the detachment construction. Excluding the constructions to be studied in sections 6.1 and 6.2 below, the LDs which remain are the NP-detachments with anaphors other than *ce/ça*, the majority of which are with one of the subject clitics *il(s)/elle(s)*.

In a sense, the latter type presents the most interesting problem for pragmatic analysis since, first of all, there is an alternation, in the discourse studied here as well as in most types of discourse, between these LD constructions and comparable constructions without LD, i.e. utterances with lexical NP subjects. Secondly, it is evident from the outset that the pragmatic difference between these two constructions is a rather subtle one, given the fact that, especially in spoken French, the subject itself ordinarily represents the topic of the sentence, given Reinhart's notion of sentence-topic.

5.2.1. *LD and information statuses — background*

In order to address this problem, and examine claims contained in the literature in the light of the present data, some acquaintance with theoretical concepts and terminology in the area known as 'information statuses' is necessary. Unfortunately, there has been much confusion in this area, but the situation seems to be somewhat improved as of late, thanks largely to the clarifying work of Prince (1981a). The most clearcut evidence that information statuses are relevant to the appropriateness of LD constructions is the ungrammaticality of indefinite NPs of specific reference in LDs:

(69) a. Le garçon il travaille avec moi.
b. *Un garçon il travaille avec moi.
c. Un garçon travaille avec moi.

Indefinite NPs of generic interpretation are acceptable as LDs:

(70) Un garçon, ça ne travaille pas beaucoup.

Indefinite generics are like definite NPs inasmuch as their referent is assumed by the speaker to be already known to, or identifiable by, the listener. Specific indefinites, on the other hand, represent entities which are assumed to be, in Prince's (1981a) terms, 'brand new' to the hearer. Thus, it was widely observed that left-detached NPs differed from subject NPs in that the former but not the latter must be referentially definite, i.e. interpretable as referring to a known and identifiable entity (or class of entities).[24]

It was noticed fairly early on, however, that the referential definiteness condition was not adequate by itself to account for certain inappropriate uses of the LD construction. Unnatural instances of LD, as in (71) (Larsson 1979: 11) were invoked to argue for a constraint going beyond mere semantic properties to a constraint based on the status of the NP's referent in the preceding discourse:

(71) Salut Jacques! Comment ça va? La soeur de Jean-Pierre, je l'ai rencontrée au cinéma.

The apparent unacceptability of LD where there is no preceding context was taken by some to indicate that the referent of the detached NP must be previously mentioned in the discourse (cf. Hankamer 1974: 221, cited by Larsson, p.11). Others pointed out that the referent need not have been mentioned if it is a salient feature of the nonlinguistic context of the utterance. Still others observed that an utterance such as (71) is appropriate in a situation where Jean-Pierre's sister is the center of interest of the speaker and the listener, i.e. their conversations concern primarily what this person does, etc. (Larsson 1979: 11-12). As Larsson notes, what is interesting is that, when the linguistic context is reduced to a minimum, a LD imposes special conditions on the extra-linguistic context, namely that the referent be given in the sense in which Chafe uses the term, viz., that the speaker assumes that that thing is in the consciousness of the hearer at that time.

Larsson (1979: 12) goes on to draw the following conclusion:

> "Le membre disloqué doit représenter quelque chose que celui qui parle croit être familier et facilement actualisé pour l'auditeur. Il doit être un thème motivé par rapport à la situation et au contexte linguistique précédent. Si nous donnons au terme élément donné une définition suffisamment vague pour couvrir ces rapports plus ou moins directs avec le contexte, il est correct de dire qu'un membre disloqué à gauche est toujours donné. Mais il est probablement préférable de définir le terme d'une façon plus restrictive [...] et alors nous devons dire que le thème indiqué par le membre disloqué à gauche fait partie d'un répertoire de thèmes qui ont une certaine actualité dans la situation de la parole. Il est souvent, mais pas nécessairement, un élément donné par le contexte linguistique précédent."

I believe Larsson's choice of a more restrictive notion of 'given' is the most reasonable position, and her description of the LD referent as often but not necessarily given by the context is borne out by the present data. Larsson's pragmatic description of the LD referent as "un thème motivé par rapport à la situation et au contexte linguistique précédent" remains without further development, as the primary concern of her study is the syntactic analysis of detachment constructions. What I shall do in what follows is demonstrate the various particular forms that this motivation may take, and also validate the observation that the LD-referent is not always given by the previous context, even where 'given' receives a very broad interpretation. Lambrecht's recent works (1984a, 1984b) seem to retain such a claim (first made in Lambrecht 1981: 67), maintaining that LD-referents must be either given in Chafe's (1976) sense, or evoked or inferrable, in Prince's (1981a) sense.[25]

Before presenting the data, there is one more terminological problem which should be treated. The supposed constraint concerning givenness or recoverability of LD-referents is sometimes described as a constraint against 'new' referents (Lambrecht 1981: 67, 1984a: 5). There are two basic senses in which one might expect the word 'new' to be used, namely, new to the discourse, i.e. not yet mentioned in the discourse,[26] or, alternatively, assumed by the speaker to be new (i.e. not familiar or identifiable) to the listener. Neither Prince's nor Lambrecht's use of 'new' corresponds to either of these uses. Prince's 'New' includes both 'Brand-new', which corresponds to 'new to the listener', and 'New-Unused', which includes entities which are new to the discourse but identifiable by the listener. However, the latter type of referent, new to the discourse but identifiable, also occurs in the separate category of 'Inferrables', which Prince's schema represents as intermediate between 'New' and 'Evoked'. It is apparent from Lambrecht's discussion (1984a: 3) that his use of 'new' coincides with Prince's use. Since it is uncontroversial that LD-referents may not be of the Brand-New type (this claim is equivalent to the referential definiteness condition referred to above), and since Inferrables are for Lambrecht 'recoverable', the category whose status with respect to LD appears to be in question is that of 'New-Unused' referents.[27] We will see below that LD-referents of the New-Unused type are not uncommon in this corpus.

5.2.2. The data

(I) *Introduction and summary*

Table 2 shows the results of a tabulation of the information statuses of the referents of LDs of the two types NP *ce/ça* ... and NP *il(s)/elle(s)*... . Some clarification of the information status categories is necessary. The category 'Evoked' includes referents previously mentioned in the discourse and referents which are part of the situational context. With respect to previous mention, I actually define this somewhat more narrowly, namely, as previously mentioned *in the same discourse segment*, i.e. in relation to the same general topic. In other words, in the case of an NP such as *ma mère*, I do not consider it evoked if the earlier mention was in the context of another discourse-topic (and, of course, at a certain distance from the current mention). Such cases are classed as New, since their identifiability is not a consequence of the previous mention, but rather of their inferrability. The category 'New' corresponds essentially to the foregoing notion of 'new to the discourse', in that it includes any referent which is not evoked. That is, both Prince's New-Unused and Inferrables are included in the category 'New'.[28] The data confirm the observation that LDs must be referentially definite, as there are no LD referents of the category 'Brand-New'; all indefinite or partitive NPs are interpretatable as nonspecific (see sec. 5.4 below).

The third category, 'Non Discourse Referent', includes referents or expressions which do not constitute discourse referents, in the sense of Karttunen (1976). These represent a particular type of the NP *c'est* LD, illustrated in (62) above. Though this type of construction constitutes an interesting

	Evoked	New	Non Discourse Referents
NP *ce/ça*...	143 (78%)*	41 (22%)	45
NP *il(s)/elle(s)*...	34 (39%)	48 (61%)	--
Total	177 (66%)	89 (34%)	45

(*Percentages are with respect to the total of Evoked and New only, for the indicated category.)

Table 2. Information statuses of lexical LD referents with subject anaphors

and significant use of the LD construction, the information status of such expressions is unclear, and, I think, more importantly, such constructions are not relevant to the question at hand.[29]

In this corpus, one-third of all NP-LDs having subject anaphors (and having discourse referents) have referents which are new to the discourse. Interestingly, comparison of the two categories (*ce/ça* vs. *il(s)/elle(s)*) shows almost a reversal in the relative proportion of Evoked and New from one type to the other; I shall comment on this below. The proportion of total Evoked to total New is virtually unchanged if we add in the remaining categories of NP-LDs, i.e. those with nonsubject (but clitic pronoun) anaphors, and those with no anaphor in the accompanying clause. It is interesting that in the latter category, Evoked and New occur in approximately equal proportions (18 Evoked, 20 New), while in the former category, Evoked referents predominate (22 Evoked, 6 New); these patterns are no doubt related to the particular nature of each of these types of LDs, and will be considered below. Given, however, that these LDs generally accomplish the same kinds of pragmatic functions as those with subject anaphors (though the relative frequencies of various functions may differ for each type), we may have occasion to draw on data from any of the categories of NP-LDs during this discussion of LD referents and information statuses.

(II) *LD with evoked referents*

Before going on to look at the particular kinds of New LD-referents and the contexts in which they occur, let us look more closely at the more typical Evoked category. First of all, there are very few cases where the LD-referent is situationally evoked, as in the following:

(72) *Votre sucre*, on dirait d'la neige. (Sugar bowl is on the table where speakers are seated.) (III,10,12)
(73) (looking at a flyer advertising French films on campus)
"*The Pain in the Neck*", c'est "l'Emmerdeuse"? (II,21,17)
(74) (pointing to a part of the above-mentioned flyer)
Celui-là, il est pas bien? (II,25,21)

Interestingly, objects in the immediate nonlinguistic context are more often introduced into the discourse by means of a right detachment construction than by a lefthand one, e.g.:[30]

(75) Il est bon, *ce thé*. (III,21,21)
(76) C'est bon, *ces popcorns*! (III,54,18)

The category of textually evoked referents in fact covers a certain range of particular types of contexts which are distinguishable by the following three criteria: (1) length of the interval between the last previous mention

Type	Time of previous mention	DT status before current mention	'Given' status before current mention
1	Very recent (usually the same or the preceding utterance)	Not a DT	Not given
2	Recent (usually within a few utterances)	Already a DT	Not given
3	Some time earlier, in same discourse-segment (usually more than a few utterances intervening)	DT following earlier mention, but not just before current mention	Not given
4	Very recent (same as Type 1)	Already a DT	Already given

Table 3. Contexts of LDs with textually evoked referents

of the referent and the LD; (2) whether the referent has the status of discourse-topic before its occurrence in the LD; and (3) whether the referent is 'given' before the LD.[31] Table 3 shows how four types of contexts which occur in the corpus are distinguished by various combinations of these parameters.

Type 1, where the referent has just been mentioned but is not yet established as a topic of the discourse, is no doubt the most frequent type. A fairly reliable indicator of topic or nontopic status is whether the previous mention occurs in subject or nonsubject position. (77) is typical in that the previous mention occurs in postverbal position:

(77) (DT = musical activities and the problems of disturbing others with practice)
M: Et là, y a pas d'problèmes pour déranger les voisins, c'est pas comme (?)
B: Oui oui, avant on avait des problèmes. C'est, c'est une des grandes raisons pour laquelle on a acheté *une maison*.
E: Pour pouvoir chanter, jouer tranquille.
B: Oui (?)
M: Non et puis *une maison* c'est pas pareil, hein, c'est tellement mieux. (I,61,15)

The previous mention and the LD may occur in utterances of the same speaker or of different speakers. (78) below (C's last turn) shows a case in which the speaker goes through the process of introducing the referent in a presentational construction (*y avait*), itself preceded by other background information, expressly in order to make a statement about the referent which constitutes a particular case of the general phenomenon under discussion:

(78) (DT = lice and the necessary treatment)
C: Faut, t'es pas obligée d'couper les cheveux, tu, tu mets de, de, un produit
E: Non, elle [=a friend] s'est pas coupée les cheveux, elle avait des cheveux mi-longs, un peu
M: Ah bon? (Je t', ma) soeur, on lui a coupé les cheveux.
C: Par contre, j'me souviens, tu sais, nous à St-Denis, c'est une, une, une région ouvrière, y a beaucoup d'immigrés et y avait beaucoup d'Portugais, et euh, *tous les Portugais*, au moment des poux, tu vois, que, que y avait une épidémie dans l'école, ils avaient, ils avaient tous la tête rasée. (III,59,23)

In the Type 2 context, the LD-referent is already a topic of the discourse in the immediately preceding discourse. It is not, however, given, which accounts for the use of the lexical NP rather than a pronominal anaphor.[32] Type 2 occurs in contexts where there are two or more primary DTs, i.e. notably in narratives (with more than one 'character') and in comparative contexts. It is of course at the points at which the center of attention, or givenness, shifts from one character to another that LD tends to occur. (79) illustrates a Type 2 context in a narrative segment:

(79) (C. is recounting a childhood summer camp excursion to the Roquefort cheese caves.)

...alors tu sais ça faisait comme un, comme un cercle quoi, comme un "O", alors on passe comme ça et pis alors y avait le, la femme, la guide, le guide quoi qui nous disait "vous voyez là, c'est le four, enfin le machin." — "Ah oueh!" On voyait rien du tout! — "Oui, c'est intéressant!" Tu vois, on passe, on passe, et les moniteurs qu'on avait, c'étaient des, bon ils étaient assez marrants quoi, ils étaient du genre à faire des conneries.

...

Bon ben i'disaient des conneries quoi, et euh, et euh, alors on passe alors très sérieux, puis on passe une fois et pis devant la guide: "Ah oui oui!", et puis alors y en a un qui commence à draguer la guide: "Ah oui oui oui, bien sûr!" On repasse une deuxième fois et puis on a passé au moins trois fois. *La guide* (ouf) elle dit: "Mais quoi? Quoi?" (I,32,5)

(80) illustrates a Type 2 context involving a comparison. The current DT concerns two variant French pronunciations of the word for 'yogurt', and whether they correspond to two different kinds of yogurt. In the case of the last LD, the referent is clearly already a topic of the discourse:

(80) C: *les yogourts*, c'est, c'est les, c'est plus liquide et le, *les yaourts*, c'est plus solide.
E: *Le yogourt*, si t'aimes mieux, c'est, c'est beaucoup plus, c'est pour végétariens, tu vois. (II,62,2-3)

In Type 3 of the textually evoked referent, the LD is separated from the last previous mention of the referent by a greater interval than in Type 2. Though the referent was a DT following its earlier mention, it is no longer so in the discourse immediately preceding the current mention. Thus, the

LD serves the function of recall or reintroduction of the earlier topic (cf. Keenan and Schieffelin 1976: 243). A plausible hypothesis is that the greater the prominence of the DT in its previous occurrence, the greater is the distance by which the later occurrence may be separated from the earlier one. It should be noted, moreover, that the earlier and the later occurrences are found within a discourse-segment which, at some level, has a common DT. For example, the following occurs within a long discourse-segment concerning M's palmreading ability; several minutes earlier in the same segment, M. recounted how she had seen in a person's palm a future affliction of madness:

>   (81) (M. has been discussing her attitude toward this ability, and the reactions of other people)
>   M: Non mais tu vois, par example, [name of individual]. *La folie*, c'est une chose que je n'ai jamais vue dans une main. (III,75,3)

The corpus also contains a certain number of tokens where the LD-referent is not only evoked and a topic of the discourse, but also is already given, viz. Type 4. That is, a pronominal anaphor would be sufficient, but the speaker uses a NP-LD. While this type is much less frequent than the preceding type, it is by no means exceptional. In these cases, the pragmatic function of the LD is the same as that described by Keenan and Schieffelin (1976: 245) for comparable cases in English, namely, it gives special emphasis to the entity already under discussion. A typical case is that where the preceding utterance is a question requesting identification or explanation of the LD-referent, e.g.:

>   (82) (previous DT = summer camp experiences)
>   E: Eh ben moi j'ai été cheftaine, mais enfin, c'était un peu différent, c'était pas, pas trop difficile.
>   C: Qu'est-ce que c'est cheftaine?
>   E: *Cheftaine*, tu sais, c'est le mouvement des guides de France.
>   (II,28,2)

In this case, the prior givenness of the LD-referent is clearly indicated by the lower pitch of *cheftaine* in C's question. E's use of the NP where *c'est* alone would have been sufficient is very typical of identification contexts; the use of the NP seems to confirm the referent as the DT, while perhaps also stengthening the association between the given expression and the equivalent expression following *c'est*. Other instances are more typical of the kind of function usually associated with emphasis, i.e. having some affective connotation or special expressive effects. For example:

(83) (DT = speakers' experiences of the baccalaureat exam)
E: Le latin, ça a pas été terrible, hein.
M: Tu as eu du latin, toi?
E: Oui oui, j'ai eu aussi du grec.
C: Ah, c'est bien.
E: C'était, alors *le grec*, c'était, c'était affreux.
M: Oh la la
E: J'ai, je crois qu'j'ai eu
C: Alpha, Beta, hein!
E: J'ai eu, oui c'est ça, j'ai eu, attends, j'ai dû avoir quelque chose comme 4 sur 20 ou un truc comme ça. Heureu-, oh le grec, là, j'en pouvais (plus). Alors *le grec* c'était horrible!
(II,41,18)

(84) (M. has just recounted a story about a friend upsetting a merchant's goods in the street.)
M: Non, mais il était malade un peu mental(-), hein, il a eu des suites
E: Ah, tes amis (ils) sont (?)
M: Oui, mais *mes amis*, je les choisis. (I,35,2)

(III) *LD with new referents*

We turn now to the one-third of the NP-LDs whose referents are new to the discourse. These may be further described, in Prince's terms, as Inferrables or New-Unused. These two types occur with approximately equal frequency, so that the New-Unused type constitutes about one-sixth of all NP-LDs in the corpus (excluding Non Discourse Referents). New-Unused referents are comprised of proper nouns or specific definite NPs assumed to be familiar to the listener, and definite and indefinite generics. The following are representative:

(85) (speakers are reminiscing about various parts of their baccalaureat exams; C. has just recounted how she did poorly in the English test)
E: Non, la philo aussi, c'était
C: La philo, c'était bon.
E: C'était bon, hein!
M: C'était
C: Ma meilleure note!
M: C'était plutôt le grand sujet. J'prenais (pas)

E: *Le latin* ça a pas été terrible, hein!
M: T'as eu du latin, toi? (II,41,10)

(86) (DT = the advantage of having an extra room in one's apartment)
E: Et puis c'qu'y a, bon ben, André euh, c'est un musicien, alors tu comprends, quand il pratique la guitare!
M: Ah, lui aussi!
E: Tiens!
M: Parce que *Ed* c'est un musicien! (I,7,15)

I do not see any sense in which the above LD-referents can be construed as recoverable or predictable (cf. Lambrecht 1981: 67, 1984a: 4-5). The fact that, in spite of having nonrecoverable referents, none of these LDs results in any sort of abruptness or discontinuity in the flow of the discourse, is attributable to what Larsson refers to as the contextual motivation of the referent, or the fact that it has "une certaine actualité dans la situation de la parole" (12). This quality of relatedness to the discourse situation is described more precisely by Reinhart (1982: 19) as one of the two types of linking devices required for discourse cohesion, namely, referential linking:

> "Two adjacent sentences are considered referentially linked if any of the following hold: the two sentences contain a mention of the same referent, or there are set-membership relations between their referents, or a referent mentioned in the second sentence belongs to the 'frame of reference' established in the first."

As a preliminary comment on the Reinhart description of referential links, it should be noted that, at least for the kind of discourse studied here, and probably for other types as well, the domain for the operation of the links needs to be widened, in some cases, to a discourse-segment larger than the sentence (or utterance). For instance, consider the following excerpt in relation to the third type of referential linking ('frame of reference' relation):

(87) M: Vous savez, Mme Barnes, du reste, ça me pose des problèmes. J'enseigne des cours de cuisine à St-Paul et les Américains à qui j'enseigne veulent toujours savoir "How many teaspoons?" "Did you say that was a, well I think that's more than a teaspoon, actually maybe it's a tablespoon." Ah oui! Alors là, moi je n'ai pas de proportions dans mes recettes.
...
E: Et puis c'qu'y a, i'faut tout, i'faut tout traduire, alors bon *le four*, c'est en Fahrenheit, tu sais jamais, tu sais jamais à quoi ça correspond (I,36,2)

The NP *le four* is a new inferrable referent which belongs to the frame of reference 'cooking', which is established not by the preceding sentence (*i'faut tout traduire*) nor by any single sentence of the preceding discourse, but rather by the entire preceding discourse-segment.

As to the application of Reinhart's description to the present data, the corpus includes LD-referents corresponding to each of the three types of referential links. The first type, recurrence of the same referent, is of course represented by the very frequent case where the LD referent has been recently mentioned in the preceding discourse. (We shall see below, in addition, that there are some cases of LD where the LD-referent is new to the discourse, but cohesion is maintained by the continuity of some other referent in the same utterance.) The second type of referential link, the set-membership relation, is noted by Galambos (1980: 129) as the second most frequent type of relation between a LD referent and its 'antecedent' (Galambos considers a LD-referent in this kind of context to be recoverable). Though Galambos does not indicate just how frequent this type is, it is apparently considerably more frequent in her corpus (Queneau's *Zazie dans le métro*) than in mine. In particular, the present corpus shows very few examples where the two referents are lexically identical (e.g. *c'est un malabar, mais les malabars c'est toujours bon*), and these are less frequent, in *Zazie* as well, than cases without lexical identity. An example of the set-membership relation which is typical of the present corpus is the following:

(88)   E: Ah moi j'trouve que les protestants sont bien plus stricts.
           B: Oui mais y a quand même des degrés de protestants aussi.
           E: Oui c'est ça. On peut parler, *les baptistes* euh, c'est un, c'est, ça va, c'est plutôt des protestants, eh bien, alors là
           M: Moi le, le, *le luthérianisme, le luthérianisme* de ma connaissance, c'est libéral.
           E: Ils sont, il faut s'accrocher hein, parce que ici, j'ai rencontré une famille, oh la la!
           C: Oui.
(I,71,7)   M: Et alors *les mormons*, qu'est-ce que c'est?

Here, each of the underlined LDs refers to a particular sect of Protestantism, which is the DT established in the preceding segment. That this kind of pattern should be frequent in this corpus is no doubt due to the nature of the corpus, namely, free conversation between a number of participants. In this kind of discourse setting, speakers typically do what Brown and Yule

(1983: 84) refer to as 'speaking topically'; that is, each one makes a contribution relating to the current DT, based on their own particular experiences or knowledge of that topic, and these contributions tend to lead to frequent changes in the DT.

As a final note on LDs and the set-membership relation, note that the relation can operate in the direction member-to-set, as well as set-to-member:

(89)   B: Mais qu'est-ce que vous mangez alors, pas de fromage?
        C: Des hamburgers!
        M: On mange américain.
        C: On s'américanise, oui.
        M: Des poulets. C'est pas cher, le poulet ici. Et puis moi j'ai au moins quatre recettes de poulet.
        C: Mais *la viande* elle est pas chère en général ici.   (I,25,12)

In a sense, the set-membership relation is but a special case of the third type of referential link, where the new referent belongs to a 'frame of reference' established in the preceding discourse. A frame of reference need not, of course, take the form of a namable set of entities, nor is it necessarily explicitly mentioned in the preceding discourse. Many of the LD-referents which are new to the discourse fit into this category. We have already seen that this is the case for (87) above. (85) also belongs to this category. In (85), the NP *le latin*, which actually refers to E's performance on the Latin portion of her baccalaureat exam, belongs to the frame of reference 'baccalaureat exams' which is the DT of a long segment of the discourse preceding this utterance.[33]

It is evident that this 'frame of reference' type of referential link subsumes Keenan and Schieffelin's (1976) LD functions of introducing a particular case of a general phenomenon under discussion or an alternative referent with respect to one previously specified with respect to some predication. A significant proportion of the 'new' LD-referents occur in this kind of comparative context. For example, in (85), the LD-referent is one of a number of different topics of the baccaleareat exam with respect to which the speakers are comparing their experiences.

There are, however, numerous instances of new LD-referents which occur in contexts which are not describable as comparative but which do fit the description of the 'frame of reference' type of referential link. For example, in some cases the new LD-referent belongs to a preestablished frame, but neither the LD-referent nor the accompanying predication are in a clear comparative relation to any preceding referent or predication; rather, the new referent and the predication provide further information, explanation, or comment on the current DT. For example, the following excerpt comes from a segment concerning M's teaching in a cooking school and, more generally, Mediterranean cuisine; M. has just revealed that it was her father who taught her to cook as a child:

(90) M: Depuis l'âge de, c'est pour ça que j'ai été embauchée du reste dans cette euh, dans cette école parce que j'ai pas de diplômes, (?) rien. J'ai jamais été chef-cuisinier ni rien.
E: Oui mais ça c'est pas, le diplôme n'a rien à voir avec euh
M: Oui oui *la femme* euh elle m'a donné euh, comment on appelle ça, euh
E: Elle t'a donné
M: Une séance d'essai avec des gens, un vrai cours et puis alors quand elle a vu ça ... (I,39,14)

The referent of *la femme* has not been mentioned anywhere in the previous discourse. The referent is identifiable, and the utterance is cohesive, by virtue of the fact that the frame of reference of a small private cooking school can plausibly be assumed to include a woman as director or manager; i.e. the referent is inferrable from other referents evoked in the preceding discourse. The following excerpt likewise includes a LD-referent which is inferrable and which has not been mentioned anywhere in the previous discourse:

(91) (DT = the extreme amount of graffiti in the New York subways, as observed by E. during a trip there)
C: Sur les banquettes aussi?
E: Non, non non. Tu vois, à l'extérieur des wagons et à l'intérieur.
C: Parce que à Paris, y a quand même des banquettes qui sont pleines de graffiti
M: Ah ben *les vandaux*, y a pas d'quoi s'ennuyer alors! (II,75,15)

For listeners with even minimal knowledge of New York City, vandals can be assumed to belong to the frame of reference of New York or New York subways which is established in the preceding discourse. The following example is comparable to the two preceding ones, except that I would argue that the referent of the LD-expression, '*alors*', is New-Unused rather than Inferrable, primarily because of its specificity (i.e. one could infer test questions on vocabulary words from the language class frame of reference, but not the particular word *alors*):

(92) E: Ah ben tiens! (C'est ce que) un de mes étudiants m'a posé la question, pourquoi on met des accents. Alors, j'lui donne l'example, (tenez), j'lui mets un mot au tableau, alors j'(lui) prononce sans accent et avec accent.
C: Mais moi c'est pareil, y en a qui m'mettent, euh, au lieu d'la Côte d'Azur, la Côté d'Azur.
E: Côté d'Azur.
C: Alors j'leur dis, ben, voilà un excellent example de la faute que vous avez faite. Maintenant, pensez aux accents!
M: Mais j'comprends pas.
E: Ben tiens, moi, finalement j'ai été surprise, *'alors'* ça a très bien passé. (II,26,6)

E. is here referring to a word in the dictation of a recent quiz they gave their classes. Though neither that word nor the particular quiz in question have been mentioned, the referent belongs to the frame of reference of classroom activities, and particularly students' spelling errors, which is established, and particularly students' spelling errors, which is established in the segment shown above. Note, however, that the presence of introductory material (*Ben tiens moi, finalement j'ai été surprise*) helps to reduce the abruptness of what would otherwise be a fairly sudden change in topic.

In all the examples considered so far, the new LD-referent itself is in some way referentially linked to the preceding discourse. There are, however, a significant number of cases where there is no referential link beteween the LD-referent and the preceding context. There are essentially two possibilities: either there is a referential link with some expression in the accompanying predication, or it is a question of Reinhart's second type of cohesive link, namely, a semantic link. The first case is represented by the following:

(93) C: [...] J'ai même eu des poux quand j'étais p'tite.
E: Non, j'ai pas eu ça non plus.
C: Alors ça, les poux, (j'avais) alors moi j'avais des (petits) poux, (hein)
M: (Les) poux, c'était à l'école. *Ma soeur* elle en avait toujours, oui. (III,59,14)

(94) (M. is recounting the story of the movie 'Madame Rosa'.)
[...] c'est, c'est vrai en plus, l'histoire, c'est pour ça qu'il a gagné le Prix. Enfin, c'était en, euh, *Nancy* elle aimerait beaucoup ça, c'était en, en argot, y avait énormément d'argot dedans [...] (II,71,6)

(Nancy is a mutual friend who is particularly well-versed in French slang.) Here the referential links are the anaphoric pronouns *en* in (93) and *ça* in (94). Here, therefore, the link between the detached NP and the preceding context is only indirect and subsequent to its occurrence; there is nothing in the previous context that suggests the likelihood of the occurrence of these particular NPs.

A semantic link is a link between propositions which occurs when "two sentences can be appropriately linked by an overt, or easily recoverable semantic connector" (Reinhart 1982: 20). Once again, I would enlarge the domain of the cohesive link to a discourse-segment, the sentence (or utterance) being the minimal such segment. I refer the reader to example (86) above, which represents a special case of the semantic link in that the predication accompanying the LD is identical to a preceding proposition. Again, the LD-referent is entirely new to the discourse and quite unpredictable. The unexpressed but easily recoverable semantic connector in this case is of course *aussi*. This kind of case also corresponds to Keenan and Schieffelin's 'alternative referent' function. Another typical case corresponds to their 'particular case' function; i.e. the implicit semantic connector is *par exemple*. For instance, the following occurs within a segment having as the DT' the earlier expressed proposition, "les couleurs de Noël, rouge et vert, c'est beaucoup plus important ici qu'en France".

(95) (previous DT = the fact that in France a poinsettia is an appropriate gift at any time of the year)
Et puis, et puis alors, *le le le grand patron de mon mari*, la semaine de Noël, il porte son costume de Noël. (I,18,18)

This LD-referent is inferrable, but entirely new to the discourse; both the LD-referent and the accompanying predication are of course completely unpredictable. The same unpredictability characterizes the LD and its predication in the following excerpt:

(96) (DT = childhood diseases that each one had)
M: Ma soeur a tout eu, elle était toujours malade, et moi je, j'étais toujours en vadrouille, à embêter les voisins.
C: T'es forte alors.
M: Robuste!
C: *Ma maman* elle dit toujours que j'ai poussé comme un champignon. (III,52,26)

There clearly is a semantic link between this predication and the previous discourse, since the predication relates to the DT of the speakers' childhood health. I suppose the implicit semantic connector would be the spoken French equivalent of English, 'in my case', namely a *moi*-LD.

If I have perhaps cited more exampes than necessary in this last part, it is in order to establish beyond a doubt that LDs with referents which are new to the discourse (even given Lambrecht's more restrictive version of the latter) are by no means a marginal phenomenon. That they are entirely acceptable is due to the other factors which assure cohesion and which are independent of the information status of the LD-referent. By showing the variety of ways in which an utterance with a LD may be related to the preceding discourse, I hope to have demonstrated that the LD structure is not significantly different in this respect from utterances with nondetached NP subjects. Are we to conclude then that the only difference between LD-NPs and subject NPs is that the former cannot be referentially indefinite, i.e. having a referent which is not identifiable by the listener? Some further considerations are necessary, before giving an answer to this question.

5.2.3. *LD and the* ya-*cleft*

Lambrecht (1981: 62) states that not all definite NPs can be left-detached because the referents of LD-expressions "can never be foci of new information". Lambrecht defines the focus as "the highlight of the new information contained in the clause" (1984: 3), and as "that element in the clause by which the new information expressed in the proposition differs most from the informational state (knowledge) the addressee was assumed to be in before the S was uttered" (1984b: 5). Lambrecht (1981: 62) gives the following illustrative contrast:

(97) (A and B are in a room. Neither A nor B have been thinking or talking about B's father. A looks out the window and sees B's father waiting outside.)
 a. #Ton père il-attend devant la porte.
 b. Y-a ton père qu'attend devant la porte.

That is, the LD is pragmatically unacceptable, and the presentational *y-a* (Standard *il y a*) construction would be used instead. Lambrecht (1981: 62) claims that (97a) is unacceptable for essentially the same reason that specific indefinites are unacceptable, i.e. because the LD-referent is not 'given'. This explanation, however, is clearly insufficient, given the numerous examples of LDs with new referents attested in this corpus.

In fact, (97a) does not appear to be an appropriate illustration of the constraint in question, since it is difficult to construe *ton père* as the focus of new information; the subject and predicate constitute equally new information in the absence of any presuppositions. A more appropriate illustration would be the case where A and B are aware of someone's presence at the door, in which case the (b) example should of course be with a *c'est* cleft rather than the presentational *y-a*, viz. *c'est ton père qu'attend devant la porte*. In the following discussion, I will attempt to elucidate the pragmatic principle underlying the distinction shown in (97) between LD and the presentational *y-a* construction, which I will call, following Lambrecht (1984a, 1984b) the *ya*-cleft.

The pragmatic distinction between LD and the presentational *ya* construction is developed in Lambrecht (1984a) and (1984b), where the claim is made that there is a pragmatic constraint on spoken French subjects to the effect that they must be both sentence-topics and given. In light of this constraint then, LD is seen by Lambrecht as a device for promoting the LD-referent from the status of recoverable to given, in order to conform to the givenness requirement on subjects. The *ya* construction is seen as having a similar function with respect to this pragmatic constraint, with the difference that the *ya* construction operates on *nonrecoverable* referents. While I think that this analysis is essentially correct, I fear that Lambrecht goes a bit too far in emphasizing the differences between LD and the *ya* construction. Though my study of the *ya* construction is so far quite limited, I would like to make some preliminary observations.

Lambrecht notes in his discussion (1984b: 9) that the *ya* construction may introduce into the discourse either a 'Brand-New' referent (i.e. a specific indefinite) or a 'New-Unused' one (i.e. definite but new to the discourse). Given the data of the present corpus, it appears then that there must be some overlap in the functions of LD and the *ya*-cleft, namely with respect to the 'New-Unused' referent type. I will illustrate here what I see as two kinds of cases. In the one, the two constructions appear to be more or less interchangeable. In the other, where this is not the case, the distinction between the two apparently has to do not with the information status of the NP-referent, but rather with the degree of cohesion between the utterance as a whole and what has preceded it in the discourse.

With respect to the interchangeability of LD and the *ya*-cleft, consider the following examples from the corpus:

>   (98)   Tu sais qu'une fois, je, j'ai j'ai j'ai, j'ai visité les caves de Roquefort, et alors qu'est-ce que je m'étais marrée. On était avec

une, j'étais en colo. Et alors *y avait toute la colo t'sais que, qui visitait*. Alors on était p't-être trente, tu vois, c'était un camp itinérant et euh, bon dans notre, dans notre périple, on est passé par Roquefort. [...] Et alors bon, on commence à passer comme ça, on fait l'tour, alors tu sais ça faisait comme une, comme un cercle quoi, comme un '0', alors on passe comme ça et pis alors *y avait le, la femme, la guide, le guide quoi, qui nous disait*, "vous voyez là, c'est le four, enfin le machin" [...]   (I,31,-32)

It seems to me that these utterances would be acceptable with LDs in place of the *ya*-clefts. They would be comparable to instances of LD such as *la femme* in (90) above, or *le mec* in the following:

(99) (DT = athletic parts of the baccalaureat exam)
      C: J'avais eu douze à la natation, oui.
      ...
      C: Ce qui était vraiment bien pour moi, parce que douze en natation
      ...
      C: Sans savoir plonger!
      M: Sans avoir plon-(?). On est obligé (pourtant). Non non, on est obligé de plonger!
      C: On était obligé, *le mec* il m'a poussée!   (II,38,14)

In (98), moreover, the word *colo* is mentioned in the previous clause, which would facilitate the use of LD. If there is a difference between (98) on the one hand and (90) and (99) on the other, it is one of length and elaboration. That is, (98) includes two parts of a relatively long narration, which is not the case for (90) or (99). The first part of (98) forms the introduction and scene-setting for the story to follow. Given the degree of elaboration of this narration, it is natural that the speaker uses the longer and functionally more marked *ya*-cleft construction. (One could also point to the fact that *y avait toute la colo* allows a more emphatic expression of the size of the group involved.)

I would like to make another comparison of a *ya*-cleft example from Lambrecht (1984b: 11) and a LD from this corpus:

(100) A, a Frenchman living in California, looking at the pouring rain outside:
      A: Ca sera l'été un jour?
      B: C'est pas du tout normal cette année, d'habitude il pleut moins

à cette saison.
A: Ya *mon frère* qui vient dans trois semaines et j'espère bien que ...

(101) (DT = M's secondhand sofa bed)
M: Lit deux places, (c'est extra!)
C: Parce que si tu as quelqu'un qui se (?)
E: Moi j'aime bien, tu vois, quand tu as des amis, euh, bon (euh si) qu'y ait une possibilité de toute façon
C: Oui. Oui, si *ma mère* elle vient me voir (en juin). (I,1,9)

At first glance, the two contexts appear to be quite similar, aside from the semantic difference of certainty vs. uncertainty of the expressed event. Closer examination reveals a difference in the preceding contexts which may be significant. In (100), if we look only as far as the clause in which the *ya*-cleft occurs, there is no apparent relation between that clause and the preceding discourse; the indirect relation between the two is revealed only in what follows. The LD of (101), on the other hand, may be seen as referring to a particular case of the more general phenomenon of houseguests which is a topic of the immediately preceding discourse. In other words, the LD-containing utterance of (101) may be seen as an example of a semantic link (cf. sec. 5.2.2) of the *par exemple* type.

I believe this last comparison reveals what may be an important pragmatic difference between LD and *ya*-clefts (in addition to the fact that *ya* but not LD can introduce a 'Brand-New' referent, i.e. a specific indefinite NP). That is, I have shown above that even when the LD-referent is new to the discourse (New-Unused or Inferrable), the utterance in which it occurs is clearly linked, either referentially or semantically, to the preceding discourse. I have found only two cases in the data where this is not the case. In one of these, the speaker explicitly notes the lack of cohesion, thus making it acceptable:

(102) (previous DT = cranberries; C. is looking at a wildlife magazine with pictures of cardinals)
C: Pour changer de conversation là, euh, vous savez, pourquoi est-ce qu'on dit, pourquoi est-ce que *le cardinal*, c'est l'oiseau de, de Noël? [...] (I,17,9)

(Recall also that the grammaticalization of LD in *c'est* contexts results in the occurrence of LD in pragmatic contexts where LD would not normally be expected.) In the second case, there is no connection whatsoever to the immediately preceding discourse, though the referent did occur in an earlier discourse segment:

> (103) (previous DT = tha anti-alcohol attitude of some Christians; Georges is the friend of one of the speakers, who agreed on the phone a little while before to come pick them up)
> B: Enfin, ils voient l'alcool comme l'origine de
> E: Du péché
> C: Du mal
> B: Du péché et du mal
> M: Dis donc euh, *Georges* i' va pas attendre dehors, bêtement dans la voiture? (I,80,1-5)

Note the use of the expression *dis donc*, which has as one of its functions the signalling of a change in topic.[34]

The hypothesis I propose is that when the *ya*-cleft introduces a definite NP (New-Unused), it differs pragmatically from LD in that there is generally a very low degree of cohesion between the *ya*-cleft utterance and the preceding discourse; in the absence of any preceding discourse, the NP-referent is *not* 'given' (i.e. the speaker has no reason to believe the referent is already in the hearer's consciousness). Thus, the *ya*-cleft is typical in utterances such as the following (Lambrecht 1984a: 8-9)

> (104) a. ya tante Ernestine qu'est arrivée!
> b. ya le téléphone qui sonne!

Lambrecht describes this function as 'event reporting', or as answering the nearly presuppositionless questions 'what happened?' or 'what's new?'. The notion of zero or minimal cohesion with the preceding discourse (or discourse-context) is a more general and thus more useful notion for describing the pragmatics of the *ya* construction. It is clear now why it is that, in the absence of any preceding discourse, LD is acceptable only if the LD-referent is already in the listener's consciousness; the latter situation represents a special case of the cohesion which characterizes LD-utterances. The enormously greater frequency of LD constructions compared to *ya*-clefts in this corpus attests to the fact that, in this kind of conversational situation, new topics are almost always introduced within the context of an existing discourse-topic. In other words, this type of conversation is extremely cohesive.

5.2.4. *LD vs. NP-subjects: the grounding principle*

I believe it is apparent, then, from the examples of the preceding sections, that NP-LDs in French have as one of their pragmatic functions the same function described by Keenan and Schieffelin (1976) for LD in English, namely the introduction of referents which are new to the discourse, where the referent or the containing utterance shows a relatively high degree of cohesion with the preceding discourse (or discourse-context). As far as the relative importance of this function compared to the more frequent function of promoting an evoked entity to one which is 'given', the statistics may be misleading. Recall that the latter function was more frequent with NP *c'est* ..., less frequent with NP *il/elle*... . It is natural that NP *c'est* ... would occur more often with an evoked referent, given the identification function of *c'est*; one generally only identifies something after it has already been mentioned in the discourse. If we recall that LDs of the NP *c'est* ... type are quasi-obligatory, then I think that the numerical preponderance of the evoked referent type becomes much less significant in the assessment of the pragmatic functions of LD.

I think another *caveat* implied by the foregoing discussioon is that we must be wary of drawing final conclusions on the basis of data drawn from a limited range of types of discourse. If neither Galambos nor Lambrecht found in their data any instances of 'new' LD-referents (i.e. New-Unused), it may be because of the differing nature of the corpuses they inspected, i.e., I assume, primarily narrative, and probably with a smaller number of speakers. Since we are interested in the use of language in all of its functions, we must of course look at a range of types of discourse to see what each can tell us about the particular problem at hand.

In the attempt to discover a functional distinction between NP-LDs and nondetached subject NPs, early descriptions of LD in French noted the requirement that detached NPs not be referentially indefinite (i.e. Brand-New, or not already indentifiable by the listener). However, it was generally overlooked that referentially indefinite NPs are rare even as nondetached subjects in informal spoken French. This corpus, like those examined by Lambrecht (1984b: 9), contains no instances of referentially indefinite NPs in nondetached subject position. In fact, comparison of detached and nondetached subject NPs in this corpus shows no difference in the possible information statuses of the referents in these two groups: in both cases, the referent may be already evoked or new to the discourse (Inferrable or New-Unused) and is never Brand-New. So, whatever functional difference distinguishes detached and nondetached subject NPs, it clearly is not a difference in the inherent pragmatic status of the referent.

While earlier treatments of LD in French did note the association of LD and the status of discourse-topic (Galambos 1980; Lambrecht 1981), it is only in Lambrecht 1984a and 1984b that this property is proposed as a systematic principle distinguishing NP-LDs and lexical NP subjects. This correlation is proposed by Lambrecht as a qualification to his proposed constraint on Spoken French subjects which requires that the latter be both sentential topics and given. The existence of clear counterexamples to this constraint in the form of lexical NP subjects is countered by the qualification that this constraint tends to operate only in foregrounded portions of a discourse. Thus, states Lambrecht, lexical NP subjects tend to be limited to backgrounded parts of the discourse. (In a more recent version of his paper, Lambrecht gives much greater importance to the degree of topicality the referent has in the discourse, than to the foreground/background distinction. He notes that the difference in topicality between NP-LDs and lexical NP subjects "often correlates with the difference between foregrounded and backgrounded parts of the discourse.")

Hopper and Thompson's (1980) definition of the foreground/background distinction, to which Lambrecht refers, has already been cited in sec. 3.6.2 above, along with some problems in its application to conversation, and some apparent counterexamples. As noted there, Lambrecht's proposal is quite adequately confirmed by the data of this corpus: the large majority of lexical NP subjects in the corpus are clearly describable as belonging to backgrounded parts of the discourse, and the large majority of NP-LDs appear to be foregrounded. Counterexamples to this principle appear to be explainable by various other factors to be noted below.

Examples of nondetached lexical subjects are found in (105) and (106):

(105) (DT = a Middle Eastern restaurant)
Non, mais c'est un bon restaurant au point d'vue nourriture et (?) là. Et c'est un Palestinien, et *les Palestiniens* sont exploités, c'est vrai, mais ils savent aussi exploiter. (III,42,14)

(106) (DT = the Place du Tertre)
Eh bien tu vois, c'est ma, ma, *une de mes grand-tantes* habitait pas loin d'la Place du Tertre, c'qui fait, alors on allait donc à Paris avec Maman pendant l'hiver. [...] [recounts having portraits done at the Place du Tertre] [...] et j'en garde un excellent souvenir,

quand on était, quand on était jeune, on allait tout l'temps à Paris. Euh, après, *ma grand-tante* est morte, alors euh, bon, on y allait moins souvent [...] (III,48,5-7)

In (105), the utterance containing the lexical NP subject is parenthetical in nature. In (106), the utterance containing the first instance provides background information, while the second also involves background information explaining the cessation of the activity which is the focus of the discourse.

Many more examples could be cited which are in accord with the foreground/background principle. What I would like to do instead is to look at a few problematic examples, to point out some possible refinements in the statement of the principle, and to see what other factors are operating in addition to this principle.

Lambrecht's description (1984b: 17) suggests that the occurrence of a NP in a foregrounded or backgrounded part of the discourse entails a higher or lower degree, respectively, of topicality. That is, NPs in foregrounded portions will be DTs, while those in backgrounded portions will not be DTs. Some examples, however, suggest that these two are in fact separate parameters which may vary independently. Moreover, the data suggests that either one of the conditions of occurring in a backgrounded discourse segment, or not having the status of a DT, is sufficient to occasion the use of a lexical subject NP rather than a LD.

One type of example supporting the independence of these two factors shows lexical NP subjects in contexts which do not appear to be background, but where the referents do not have the status of DTs. Consider, for example, the following segment, where the DT is Martine's apartment:

(107) E: Alors, t'as deux chambres? Tu as deux chambres? (euh)
M: Une grande salle à manger
E: Une grande salle à manger, une cuisine et une salle de bains
M: Voilà, c'est ça, et puis *la chambre d'invités* est quand même grande, et *notre chambre* est immense, à nous. On a deux immenses placards (I,4,16-19)

That the referents of the underlined NPs do not have the status of DTs is indicated by the fact that they do not reoccur (as NPs or pronouns) in the succeeding discourse. Yet I do not see any indication that the containing utterance is background, as it seems to me that it does contribute directly to the speaker's goal, namely the description of the apartment and, in particular, the ample space it provides. Here, the nontopicality of the given NPs appears to follow not from the backgrounded nature of the containing utterance, but rather from the fact that they refer to only parts of the whole (the apartment) which is the DT, and no one part is of any special interest in itself.

Another even clearer example of the occurrence of a nontopical referent in a segment which does not appear to be background occurs in a description of the game called *la balle aux prisonniers*:

(108) C: Alors, y a deux équipes, ça fait comme un, une équipe d'un côté, l'autre équipe de l'autre. On a une balle et avec la, on essaie de toucher
E: De toucher le
C: les, les gens de l'équipe
E: De l'équipe adverse
C: adverse. Une fois qu'*la personne* est touchée, elle va dans le camp du prisonnier de l'équipe adverse
M: Oui, c'est ça
E: Et elle essaie, pour se libérer, elle a l'droit de prendre la balle et de toucher la per-, une personne de l'équipe, euh
E: (qui l'adverse) qui l'a, qui l'a
E&C: qui l'a fait prisonnière.
C: Et si elle touche quelqu'un, elle peut retourner dans son camp et rejouer. (Si elle) ne touche pas quel-, si elle ne touche personne, elle reste dans le camp de prisonniers et jusqu-, et jusqu'à ce que la balle dépasse le, le, le camp de, adverse. Si tu veux parce que il faut tout l'temps rattraper la balle, il faut jamais que la balle tombe. Enfin, plus ou moins. Et si la balle va trop loin, alors à ce moment-là, elle, *la balle* appartient au camp des prisonniers et à ce moment-là, c'est, excusez-moi, c'est là où ils euh, c'est à ce moment-là que les prisonniers peuvent tenter un autre euh, une autre
M: Sortie
C: sortie euh, quoi.
E: Mais comme tu (vois)
M: C'est un jeu vraiment rapide, c'est vraiment rapide.
E: Ah oui! (Mais quand tu veux) quand tu veux essayer d'toucher ton adversaire, *la balle*, des fois, ne touche pas, elle va très loin et c'est pour ça qu'elle va dans l'camp des, de ceux qui sont prisonniers.[35] (II,29,7-20)

Though the referent *la balle* is mentioned nine times after its initial mention, only two of these mentions (the last two) are in pronominal form. In the last turn, *la balle* does seem to acquire a somewhat greater degree of topicality, as indicated by the two pronominal anaphors, but if it were truly a topic of the discourse, then one would expect a LD in place of the lexical NP subject in this turn. Clearly more topical than *la balle* is the other main discourse entity of the passage, *la personne*. *La personne* is followed by eight pronominal anaphors, and four of these are subjects of main clauses. Of the six occurrences of *la balle* in C's long turn, three are in subordinate clauses and two are direct objects; both of these environments are of course associated with nontopical referents (Lambrecht 1984b: 18, 27-28). Low agentivity, another correlate of low topicality, also distinguishes *la balle* from *la personne*. Note that although *la personne*, at least in C's longer turn, is more topical than *la balle*, I would argue that it still does not attain the level of topicality required to be considered a DT. Notice that the first and only occurrence of the lexical NP *la personne* is in an utterance-initial subordinate clause (*Une fois qu'* ...), an environment which is most atypical of topical referents. The fact that *la personne* does not attain the status of a DT may be attributed to its nonspecific nature (Lambrecht 1984b: 18,23-26). I believe there is also a parallel between this example and the preceding one, in that *la personne* and *la balle* are simply participants in, or components of, the game scenario which is itself the topic of this discourse segment.

Having established the relatively low topicality of the discourse entities of this segment, the remaining question is whether the segment is background or foreground. Once again, I can see no indication that it is background, i.e. that it "merely assists, amplifies, or comments on [the speaker's goal]" (Hopper and Thompson 1980: 280); rather, it seems to me that it does "immediately and crucially contribute to the speaker's goal", which is in this case the description of the game *la balle aux prisonniers*.

These departures from the usual background-low topicality correlation are examples of the kinds of problems which arise from the attempt to apply to conversational discourse a principle originally proposed for narrative discourse. The two cases cited here both involve description.[36] In Hopper's (1979) exposition, descriptive discourse is clearly background, as it does not serve to advance the main story line. Of course, in free conversation, there is most often no story line with reference to which the foreground/background distinction can be made. It is not clear on what alternative criteria, if any, this distinction might be based for nonnarrative discourse, aside from the more general language used in Hopper and Thompson (1980), referring to the nature of the contribution to the "speaker's goal". By that criterion, I think the two passages just examined must be considered to be foregrounded.

Lambrecht's discussion (1984b: 31) suggests the possibility of the independence of grounding and topicality, in a case where the referent is fairly topical because the narrative centers around the referent, but the referent's first mention is in a background segment at the beginning of the narrative. In this case, the referent appears as a lexical subject, i.e. its topicality is not overtly marked by a LD. The following example represents the same kind of case, except that here the referent is clearly established as the DT prior to the backgrounded portion:

(109) E: (?)tu es comme, tu es comme mon père. *Moi mon père* il est terrible. Quand Maman fait un gateau
C: Mais j'ai même pas faim, hein!
E: Il est un petit peu, *mon père* est grand, mais il est pas vraiment mince, hein, on peut pas dire ça, hein. Alors Maman fait un gateau, prépare quelque chose. *Mon père* dit: "Ah non! Ca, l'gateau, j'en prends pas!" Et puis après, i'dit: "Il faut quand même que j'y goûte, j'peux pas, j'peux pas lui faire ça." Alors i'prend une petite part, bon, très bien. Maman coupe des parts normales, tu vois, mais alors *lui*, il coupe sa part
M: En deux, ou (II,43,9-12)

The LD in E's first turn is typical in establishing *mon père* as DT, after its immediately prior nontopical first mention. E. then begins a narration to show how her father is "*terrible*", but interrupts herself (following C's interruption) to give some background. Notice that she first uses *il* to refer to her father, but then switches to the lexical NP, apparently believing that the referent is not yet topical enough for the pronominal reference. The nonuse of LD in this case can be attributed to the backgrounded nature of the utterance. It is not clear, however, why the following occurrence of *mon père* is not detached, as the referent appears to be fairly topical here, and an LD would be entirely acceptable. Lambrecht (1984b) suggests a possible explanation,[37] but it may be that occasional counterexamples such as this should be taken as indicating that the principle in question describes a tendency rather than a categorical rule.

To summarize so far, most of the data support the principle that a referent must be topical (in the discourse) in order to be detached, and that a nontopical referent occurring in a foregrounded portion of the discourse will still not be marked by LD. That is, occurrence in a foregrounded part of the discourse is not sufficient to promote a nontopical referent to a topical one. On the other hand, a referent which is topical in a certain discourse segment but which occurs in a smaller background portion of that segment is not normally marked as topical. Thus, while there is usually a correlation between foreground and topicality, and background and nontopicality, the grounding and topicality parameters are in fact independent. As noted above, most of the data support the principle that a referent must be both topical and foregrounded (i.e. occurring in a foreground portion of the discourse) in order to be detached.

As already suggested, the corpus contains a number of counterexamples to this principle. Most of these are cases of LD where the referent is not describable as a DT. In one case, a LD occurs in what appears to be a backgrounded portion of the discourse. The referent does not appear to be a DT, but it does have a certain degree of topicality. I think the example is interesting as an illustration of other difficulties in applying the grounding principle to conversational discourse:

(110) (M. is recounting how she wrote in a letter to her parents that her husband was taking his CIA exams, without explaining that CIA stood for Certified Internal Auditing. M. recites her father's response.)
M: "[...] ça devient sérieux, c'est une nouvelle orientation qui n'a rien à voir avec les chiffres! Et puis, et puis euh"
E: L'espionnage!
C: Oueh, oueh!
M: Oui, "et puis ta soeur," parce que *ma soeur* euh elle s'est, s'est pas mal occupée de l'OLP pendant plusieurs années, du mouvement palestinien
E: Ah oui?
M: Secrétaire des Finances, enfin, elle a fait pas mal de choses, donc euh, là on voyait déjà des problèmes américains, tunisiens qui, et euh
B: J'dois avouer que moi j'ai travaillé pour la CIA!
E: Ah, Betsy! (laughter)
M: Donnez-moi (?)
C: On va tout savoir!
E: Donnez-nous les cassettes avant d'partir!

> M: Mais (?), j'ai toujours rêvé que ma soeur soit un héros, un héros, très active. (III,84,14-22)

That the referent of *ma soeur* does not appear to be a DT, at least at its first introduction into the discourse, is indicated not simply by the preceding *parce que*; it seems to be clearly subordinated to the current topic, which is the reaction of M's parents to the news of her husband's CIA exams. M's description of her sister's activities, which seems almost parenthetical, serves to explain her father's reference to her sister. What is interesting is that M's sister appears to almost become a topic of the discourse in her own right. Notice the following pronominal reference (*elle a fait pas mal de choses*), and, what is even more interesting, M's reintroduction of the topic of her sister six lines later, after a slight 'digression'. I enclose the latter term in parentheses because the notion of digression assumes that the discourse has a predetermined purpose (or topic) and that the form of the discourse is then determined according to that goal. But of course it is the nature of free conversation that there is no predetermined goal or topic, and the form of the discourse is only created as the discourse itself develops. Though the succession of topics in a discourse usually shows a high degree of relatedness, there are clearly many more topic changes in this kind of discourse than in an extended narrative discourse, and what appears at first to be the topic of a digression (i.e. not centrally related to the previous DT) may well become the new DT. Following the excerpt cited above, there are fifteen more turns dealing primarily with B's experience at the CIA Language School, before the speakers return to the original topic of M's parents' reaction and what 'CIA' actually meant here. Clearly, the determination of the foreground or background nature of a discourse segment is considerably complicated by the constantly evolving nature of the DT in free conversation. An additional complicating factor is the fact that at any one time, various participants in the discourse may have differing notions and intentions as to what constitutes the topic of the discourse. This appears to be the case in the last turn cited above, where M. seems to be attempting to reestablish her sister as the DT.

As for the cases where the LD-referent is not a DT, most of these occurrences appear to be attributable to various other factors. The clearest case is that of NP *c'est* [...] contexts; as noted above, LD is quasi-grammaticalized in this context, and does not depend on the topic status of the referent. Several of the other cases of nontopical LDs suggest that there is a tendency for LD to occur when the initial NP is followed by intervening material such as adverbial phrases or even simple hesitation particles, e.g.:

(111) (DT = a certain kind of pastry that E's mother bought for her children when they were sick)
    E: I'faut pas les commander parce que comme *ma maman* euh elle devait pas prévoir qu'on allait être malade. (III,51,16)

(112) (M. is recounting one of her palmreading experiences.)
    M: [...] j'ai même vu des, des choses avec sa femme, les relations avec sa femme et j'ai même vu les problèmes. Alors, alors les gens évidemment s'inquiètent quand tu dis que *le problème* euh il est là, il est évident, parce que c'est cette croix ici, alors i's ont (peur) (III,69,4)

Both of these LDs occur in what appear to be backgrounded subordinate clauses and have referents which are, I think, functionally subordinated to the current DT. Though *le problème* does have two succeeding anaphoric references, notice that the referent is nonspecific, which favors low topicality. Notice that the problematic LD of (110) is also followed by a hesitation particle. (Cf. also example (90) above.

In section 5.2.2 above, we saw that LD-referents may be new to the discourse, and that there is usually, in such cases, some kind of referential or semantic link which assures cohesion between the containing utterance and the preceding utterance. It was further noted that while the majority of these cases show a referential link involving the LD-referent itself, there are also cases where the LD-referent itself is 'unmotivated' and cohesion depends on a referential link involving some other referent in the utterance, or on a semantic link. If we look at just the latter cases, where the LD-referent is 'unmotivated', we find that many of these coincide with cases where the LD-referent is not a DT (cf. examples (93), (94), (96), and (101) above). Likewise, nontopical LDs are found among cases of LD referents which are only inferrable from the frame of reference of the preceding discourse (cf. (90) and (99)). This suggests that one of the functions of LD (though admittedly a minor one) is to introduce a referent for which there is little motivation (in the sense of Larsson, cf. sec. 2.2 above) in the preceding discourse. That is, it serves to introduce a referent whose occurrence in the given context is quite unpredictable, regardless of whether or not the speaker intends for the referent to become a DT. By introducing the referent before the proposition commenting on it, the LD diminishes the effect of discontinuity otherwise produced by the occurrence, in subject position, of an 'unmotivated' referent. Several of these cases occur in turn-initial position, as in (96) above and (113), suggesting a possible additional motivation as a turn-taking device:

(113) (DT = the problem of obesity in America)
 E: [...] Parce que moi la première fois qu'j'suis arrivée, j'ai vu des, surtout les femmes, ça des fois c'est des monstres hein
 M: Mais *ma mère* elle en revenait pas, hein! (II,53,11-12)

5.3. NP-LDs with nonsubject anaphors

A few brief observations are in order concerning the group of NP-LDs which have an anaphor in the accompanying clause that is not the grammatical subject of the clause. These constitute only about 7% of all NP-LDs.[38]

As one might expect, given the distinctive pragmatic status of subjects, the pragmatic description of LDs with nonsubject anaphors is somewhat different from the one presented above for those with subject anaphors. It is first of all much more homogeneous, due to the fact that the great majority of NP-LDs with nonsubject anaphors (hereafter, NSA-LD) are with LD-referents which are Evoked. The low frequency of NSA-LDs with referents which are new to the discourse (i.e. New-Unused or Inferrable) is no doubt attributable in part to the fact that nonsubject constituents lack the inherent topicality of subjects which allows even a 'new' referent to be the topic of the sentence.[39] The same point can be rephrased by saying that nonsubjects are inherently low in topicality, where inherent topicality corresponds to Reinhart's notion of topic as 'what the sentence is about', independent of the old/new information distinction. Given this fact, then it becomes quite clear why the large majority of NSA-LDs are with evoked or even 'given' referents, as this is the principal way in which a nonsubject expression can come to represent 'what the sentence is about'.

About half of the NSA-LDs have referents which correspond to the Type 4 context of Table 3 above (p. 100). That is, they are not only evoked, but are already given as well. In other words, an anaphoric reference alone would have been acceptable in these cases. Given the redundancy of the detached NP, these naturally lend themselves to an emphatic interpretation. An example of this type has been given in (84) above. The emphatic function is not as clear in some cases, as in the following:

(114) M: Et l'examen, c'est quand qu'tu l'passes? Oui oui. C'est quand que tu passes l'examen, toi?
 E: Eh ben *l'examen*, je reviendrai euh, en automne pour le passer [...] (III,16,4)

This example is similar to Lambrecht's (1981: 63) examples (77) and (78) and to (82) above, all of which are answers to questions contained in the immediately preceding turn. I agree with Lambrecht's analysis of this type of LD as serving to establish a sort of communicative agreement between the speakers by explicitly marking the referent as the DT. These cases appear to be comparable to cases of object fronting in Spanish analyzed by Silva-Corvalan (1983) as calling the listener's attention to a referent which is old information by placing it in a position where it can receive pitch prominence.

The remaining half of the NSA-LDs, with a few exceptions to be noted shortly, correspond to the Type 2 context of Table 3. Their referents have all been mentioned in the very recent discourse, but are not sufficiently given to allow an anaphoric reference alone. That is, most of these LD-referents are already a topic of the discourse, but, for various reasons, the referent is not the center of attention, or the unique center of attention, at the narrow level of the sentence. There are two such examples in the following excerpt from a discourse-segment on the problem of obesity in America:

(115) (C. is talking about her last tap dancing lesson)
C: [...] j'ai vu mercredi et ça j'me suis dit, ça c'est drôlement bien, une femme énorme, tu vois, qui était v'nue en, à, qui était en justaucorps avec ses collants et tout, en claquettes. J'me disais, ça, en France, jamais.
E: En France, jamais!
M: Ah mais ça c'est une chose ici qui a frappé mes parents.
E: Ah oui.
M: C'est que *les gens qui ont vraiment un problème de poids, qui sont vraiment trop gros*, en été, tu les vois comme les autres, autour des lacs, en short.
C: Oui, exactement!
E: En France, jamais!
M: Oh jamais! Mais quelqu'un qui a juste quelques kilos de trop n'ose pas, n'ose pas mettre un short,
E: Ah non non non!
M: n'ose pas marcher sur la plage avec une, une jupe trop courte.
C: Mais ça c'est un, ça c'est un truc qui est bien.
E: Ca c'est positif, bon, dans un sens, parce que y a pas d'raison que, tu vois, que *les gens qui sont gros*, on les exile [...]
(II,55-56)

What makes the fronted position of these NPs natural is the fact that they represent what is presupposed by the preceding discourse, while the rest of the proposition gives some new information about them.

In the following, the use of the NP to refer to an already topical referent is required by the presence of a double DT:

(116) M: Ben moi je sais, ici hein, on est que deux à la maison, alors, quand je fais euh, du maroni, c'est un gâteau euh, un gâteau euh, Middle-Eastern là, et quand je fais, euh du couscous, parce que c'est surtout le couscous et le maroni, j'en fais comme si on était dix.
E: Tu (ne peux pas nous apporter) des parts, dans l'département?
M: Alors évidemment, *le maroni*, tu, tu vas pas l'laisser traîner, tu comprends, le, le, le lendemain, c'est moins bon. Mais on se bourre, on se bourre, et puis alors *le couscous*, on supporte pas de savor qu'il en reste [...] (II,43,20)

I mentioned above that there are a few exceptions to the generalization that these LD-referents have been mentioned in the immediately preceding discourse. These cases, comparable to the Type 3 context of Table 3, are those where the LD serves to recall to the listeners' consciousness a previous DT whose topicality has been suspended during a brief digression. Example (120) below is one of these cases. The following includes another:

(117) (M. has just recounted a childhood incident where she had to eat a dish she disliked very much.)
C: J'me souviens d'manger un boudin à quatre heures qui était froid. Oh, j'me souviendrai toujours, ça. Ma mère, on, on avait mangé du boudin, j'aimais pas l'boudin.
M: Ah oui, c'était bizarre comme consistance.
C: Je savais qu'c'était du sang. Rien que d'savoir ça, j'en, j'aimais pas l'boudin.
E: Oui c'était (?)
C: Alors, puis, tout ça, alors bon, *l'boudin*, j'tardais à l'manger,[...] (II,65,19)

Here the LD marks a return to the narrative which C. had begun before the brief digression on blood sausage in general. Notice that although the expression *l'boudin* refers to the topic of the digression, it there has a generic reading, while the detached NP refers of course to the specific sausage of this incident. These cases appear to differ slightly from the Type 3 cases of sec. 5.2.2 in that here the digression is short enough that the LD-referent retains a high degree of topicality.

Thus, NSA-LDs differ from subject-anaphor (SA) LDs not only in the near exclusion of 'new' referents. Conspicuously absent in the category of NSA-LDs is the Type 1 context of Evoked referents, which is most typical of SA-LDs, where the referent is only promoted to the status of DT with the LD. What this suggests is that the description of LD-referents which are already 'given' (i.e. the center of attention) or already topical as exceptional (cf. Galambos 1980: 127) is at best imprecise. Conversely, the description of LD in French as a topic-shifting device is valid primarily for LDs with subject anaphors, and even then there are of course 'exceptions'. Our highlighting of *particular* functions most characteristic of NSA-LDs vs. SA-LDs should not, however, obscure the basic similarity of both types, namely that the LD represents a referent to which the speaker wishes to give special prominence as a topic of the discourse, whether it be for the specific purpose of emphasizing a current topic, recalling a previous one, or establishing a new one.

Interestingly, the fact that LD-referents may be already 'given' distinguishes French from both English (Keenan and Schieffelin 1976) and, more surprisingly, Italian (Duranti and Ochs 1979: 401). The difference with English is apparently due to the fact that English uses, in the same pragmatic contexts, the structure referred to as Topicalization, i.e. a 'fronted' constituent with a zero anaphor in the clause (cf. sec. 6.1). The absence of already 'given' LD-referents in Italian is particularly surprising in view of the fact that *all* LDs in Italian are with nonsubject anaphors (due to the absence of subject clitic pronouns in the language; cf. Duranti and Ochs 1979: 380-381). On the other hand, the cases studied in this section appear to be comparable, as noted above, to certain cases of object fronting in Spanish (Silva-Corvalan 1983).

5.4. The definiteness constraint

As already mentioned, the data do confirm the well-known condition that detached NPs be referentially definite. I would like to briefly examine certain examples which illustrate certain fine points of this distinction which are insightfully observed by Larsson (1979: 28-30), specifically, cases of formally indefinite NPs which can be interpreted as semantically definite.

The most frequent case of this type is of course the singular indefinite NP of generic interpretation, as in the following:

(118) *Une boîte de nuit*, regarde combien tu dois payer! (II,81,12)

Likewise, indefinite plural or partitive NPs are possible in LD constructions:

(119) *des saunas comme* ça, y en a surtout dans le, dans le sud de la France (II,7,5)

Lambrecht (1981: 61-62) explains cases such as these by stating that the NPs "are interpreted as parts of generic wholes". But in fact, isn't this statement true of *all* instances of partitive (and even plural indefinite) NPs? Larsson's analysis is more exact; she proposes a negative formulation of the constraint to the effect that the detached indefinite NP must not be specific in reference (28). In other words, Larsson recognizes the fact that it is not a question of a simple binary distinction between generic and specific reference, but rather that there are some 'grey areas' in between. For instance, I am not at all certain that we would wish to say that the LD-expressions of (120) and (121) have any sort of generic interpretation:

(120) (current DT = Polish cuisine; borscht, or beet soup was an earlier topic of the segment)
Mais *une soupe, une soupe à la betterave*, j'en ai déjà mangé moi au (?) (I,43,10)

(121) (E. is describing the meals cooked by the dieting mother of the American family with whom she boarded)
Alors à chaque fois on avait, ah oui! Alors là, (?), *des légumes*, on en avait. On avait pas, on avait pas d'ça! (pointing to the dip they are eating with fresh vegetables) (II,51,6)

While I believe this area calls for further study, one point I believe bears noting is the extent to which the interpretation of the LD-expression may be determined by the very fact of its detachment. For example, with respect to the LDs of (120) and (121) above, it seems to me that if these NPs were in postverbal object position, they would be susceptible of an entirely specific interpretation which is not possible in the detachment construction. That is, their sentential contexts contain little in the way of lexical features that suggest a nonspecific interpretation, aside from perhaps the adverb *déjà* in (120) and the iterative aspect of (121). It seems to me that the nonspecific interpretation given to these NPs is largely a consequence of the fact that they are detached, i.e. specifically, as a consequence of the syntactic independence of the expressions and of their concomitant presupposed status. (By 'presupposed', I mean simply that the referent is presented as the topic of the clause which is to follow.) Another way of putting this notion is to recall that the LDs of (120) and (121) are functionally similar to the phrases "as for (a) beet soup" and "as for vegetables", where a specific interpretation is clearly ruled out.[40] It may appear that my description is somewhat circular, but perhaps that is precisely the point. That is, rather than looking at certain semantic properties of LD-expressions as evidence of a constraint on the LD construction, it may in some cases be more appropriate to view those properties as a consequence of the syntactic and pragmatic status of LD-expressions.[41]

Finally, the following two examples illustrate another type of case which appears at first to be problematic for the referential definiteness, or nonspecificness constraint:

(122) (DT = fellow (female) graduate students and their ages)
Moi, *une qui m'a étonnée*, c'est S. quand elle m'a dit qu'elle avait trente ans (III,67,18)

(123) (DT = funny answers given by students in their classes)
C'est comme moi. *Un*, je lui demande, est-ce que, quel est le rêve de votre vie? (II,26,16)

If we alter these LD-expressions by making explicit what is supplied by the context, i.e. giving *une [des étudiantes] qui m'a étonnée*, and *un [de mes étudiants]*, then it is clear that these NPs are of the type discussed by Larsson (1979: 29-30) and referred to by Selkirk (1977) as '*vrais partitifs*'. That is, an NP such as *une des étudiantes* differs from *une étudiante* in that, in the first case, the referent belongs to a set of individuals which is itself definite, i.e. identifiable by the listener. Thus, though the NP is clearly specific in reference, the definiteness of the group to which it belongs is sufficient to make the referent of the NP identifiable, or at least sufficiently identifiable to be acceptable as an LD (Larsson 1979: 30).

6. SPECIAL CASES

6.1. 'Topicalization' and 'Focus Movement' in spoken French

A construction often associated with LD is that referred to as 'Topicalization', that is, where a nonsubject constituent of the sentence occurs in sentence-initial position, with no anaphor being present in the sentence, as in the English sentence:

(124) *Beans* I like.

According to Chafe (1976: 49), the fronted constituent represents a focus of contrast, and there may be a second focus of contrast elsewhere in the sentence (e.g. in (124), *like* may or may not be a focus of contrast; in English, constituents which represent foci of contrast show a distinctive intonation contour, namely, they are marked by a steep fall in pitch.)

Prince (1981b) distinguishes on pragmatic grounds the two readings of (124), reserving the term 'Topicalization' for the reading with two foci of contrast, and labelling the other reading, with a single focus of contrast, 'Focus Movement'. Prince also shows that in fact, the effect of contrast is not necessarily present in either construction.

The corpus contains 22 examples of constructions like (124).[42] These examples fall into two groups which appear to correspond to the two construction types distinguished by Prince (1981b). Closer examination reveals that while the Focus Movement constructions are quite comparable to their English counterparts, the apparent cases of Topicalization should probably be considered to be special cases of LD. Moreover, certain cases of LD are observed to serve the same pragmatic function as Topicalization in English.

We will consider the Focus Movement constructions first, since they are the simpler case. They are also the smaller group, comprising four examples, of which the following are representative:

(125) C: Après, vous allez me faire sentir exclue et
M: *Impolie*, tu veux dire. (II,2,19)
(126) C: (looking at the salt and pepper shaker on the table at which they are seated) Ils sont jolis euh

M: *Une salière et une poivrière*, on dit non? (II,2,23)

In each of these cases, the fronted constituent represents the new information of the utterance, which is typically an expression used nonreferentially. The rest of the sentence is almost superfluous, functioning much like ordinary parenthetical expressions in the reporting of discourse. Note that these fronted expressions carry a specially high pitch rise, higher than that of typical LDs, while the rest of the utterance is low in pitch. These constructions are pragmatically exactly comparable to those constructions described by Prince (1981b) under the name Focus Movement.[43]

Of the eighteen no-anaphor constructions which appear to correspond to Prince's Topicalization, sixteen are with the demonstrative pronoun *ça* as the lefthand element, while only two examples have lexical NPs in initial position. As to the former, the 'fronted' *ça* is always emphatic and sometimes involves contrast. These cases appear to satisfy Prince's description of Topicalization, according to which the initial NP represents either an evoked entity or "one that is in a salient set-membership to something already in the discourse" (253), and "the open sentence resulting from the replacement of the tonically stressed constituent in the [...] proposition by a variable represents salient/given information" (258). The following examples are representative:

(127) (DT = the recipe for the vegetable dip they are eating)
  (to B) Vous en avez pas mis beaucoup, d'gingembre, parce que j'aime pas ça, et *ça* j'aime bien. (II,23,16)
(128) C: Ca c'est un truc que j'aime bien ça, dans les trucs américains, c'est qu'on mange des crudités comme ça. *Ca* j'aime bien.
  E: Mais là, tu vois, (j'aime bien, euh) j'aime bien euh la sauce, mais y a des fois où elle est un peu sucrée, alors là, *ça* vraiment, j'aime pas. (II,24,8-9)

It is significant that of these sixteen cases, more than half are with one of the verbs *aimer* (or *adorer*) or *savoir*, while a quarter are with *connaître* or *comprendre*. Notice that all of these verbs occur very frequently in spoken French with deleted or zero object anaphors, e.g. *je sais, je connais pas*. Notice the contrast between the following two examples with *savoir*, which arises because of the fact that *savoir* does not allow omission of the anaphor when the verb is in the *passé composé* (e.g. **oui, j'ai su*):

(129) a. [...] et *ça* je savais absolument pas (III,71,7)

b. [...] et *ça* je l'ai su, j'ai eu la mauvaise surprise en juin [...]
(II,80,11)

These syntactic facts, along with the pragmatic similarity of these cases of 'fronted' *ça* and *ça*-LDs, suggest that what we are dealing with here is simply a special case of LD. The two examples with lexical NPs appear to be pragmatically comparable to the preceding cases, also satisfying Prince's description of Topicalization. Notice that they occur with verbs already noted above, viz. *adorer* and *savoir*:

(130) (DT = the type of sauna found in America)
Oui mais *le sauna*, alors moi j'aime pas tellement parce qu'il y a aucune, y a pas de, tu vois, c'est sec (II,7,20)

(131) (DT = spelling errors their students make; '*alors*' was included in a dictation in a recent test)
E: Ben tiens moi, finalement j'ai été surprise, '*alors*' ça a très bien passé.
C: Oui, moi aussi.
E: Toi aussi? Hein?
C: Ils mettaient deux 'l' ou euh
E: (Oui) moi aussi, mais enfin
C: Y en a euh, j'en ai pas mal qui ont bien écrit.
E: Oui, parce que j'me suis dit, '*alors*', ha, ils vont pas savoir, ils vont, parce que j'emploie pas tellement en classe (II,26,12)

Notice that in both cases, the semantically appropriate anaphor of the left-hand NP would be *ça*. Also notice, in the last example, that the speaker omits any anaphor for *alors* in the second clause, as well as in the first one following its 'fronted' occurrence.[44]

The data suggest then that Topicalization is extremely marginal in spoken French, occurring primarily with verbs which allow zero anaphors in other syntactic contexts, and always in contexts where *ça* would be a semantically appropriate anaphor. It appears that spoken French normally requires that fronted referential NPs have an anaphor in the accompanying clause. Evidence in favor of such a constraint would be the existence of LD constructions which are pragmatically identical to the Topicalization construction of English. In fact, there are in the corpus at least two such instances, which I think are clear examples of the kind of focus of contrast often associated with Topicalization in English:

(132) (E. is describing the meals cooked by the dieting mother of the American family with whom she boarded.)
Alors à chaque fois on avait, ah oui! Alors là, (?), *des légumes*, on en avait. On avait pas, on avait pas d'ça! (pointing to the vegetable dip on the table) (II,51,6)

(I refer the reader to fn. 40 for further description of this example.)

(133) (M. is talking about a palmreading incident where she was asked by a third person if the person was a virgin.)
Oui, et c'est une chose que je ne cherche pas, si tu veux, les gens me disent toujours est-ce que j'me marie, est-ce que je serai riche, alors *ces choses-là*, je les cherche. Dans le poignet, dans, dans le petit doigt, bon, je les cherche. (III,73,14)

Both of the above LD-expressions carry a specially high pitch rise; the rest of the sentence has a normal descending contour, and the sentence-final verb carries some extra stress. Again, I believe that the LDs of (132) and (133) can be considered to satisfy, in a straightforward manner, Prince's (1981b) pragmatic description of Topicalization. Notice that these constructions recall Lambrecht's (1981) nonemphatic contrastive structure discussed in sec. 3.3. In fact, Lambrecht's pragmatic description of the contrastive detachment construction appears to be in accord with the pragmatic description of Topicalization referred to here.

The evidence from this corpus is of course too limited to draw any final conclusions, but some hypotheses are possible. First, the status of the Focus Movement construction (as in (125) and (126) above) in spoken French is unproblematic. On the other hand, there is evidence that LD in French has as one of its functions the same pragmatic function that characterizes Topicalization in English. It appears that LDs with zero anaphors should be treated as a special case of LD. If these hypotheses are correct, they furnish some evidence in support of the distinction between Topicalization and Focus Movement.

6.2. No-anaphor LDs

An LD sub-type generally neglected in the literature (Larsson 1979: 44-45 is an exception) is that where the LD expression has no anaphor in the accompanying clause (cf. fn. 42). Such constructions account for 10% of the total LDs of the corpus, with 61 instances of pronominal detachments (41 *moi*, 10 *nous*, and 9 *ça*) and 45 instances of lexical NP detachments. As suggested in sec. 2.2 above, given that the function of LD-expressions without anaphors appears to be essentially similar to that of the more frequent type, the existence of these no-anaphor LDs has important consequences for our notion of sentence-topic and the topic-comment relation. After outlining these issues, we will examine some of the no-anaphor LDs and describe how they function in the discourse.

Recall that Reinhart (1982) defines the sentence-topic as that expression of the sentence which represents the thing about which the assertion contained in the sentence is intended to expand our knowledge. (Note that this notion of topic is equivalent to what Chafe (1976) calls subject.) Reinhart further notes that this definition of topic entails the following semantic condition: "roughly, it must be possible to interpret the proposition expressed in the sentence as a property of the individual or the set denoted by the NP." (13) Given the high percentage of LDs which correspond to grammatical subjects (81% in our sample), and given the fact that French subjects usually satisfy the preceding semantic condition (interpreting *property* in a broad sense), it is clear that the large majority of French LDs are accurately described by Reinhart's notion of topic. The remaining instances (19%) are almost evenly divided between tokens with no anaphor in the clause (10%) and tokens with non-subject anaphor (9%). The latter type are also generally characterizable by this same notion of topic, since in most of these cases the direct or indirect object (corresponding to the LD) has a semantic role which could be described as highly topical. For example, where the object is animate, it commonly bears the role of experiencer, as in (134) and (135):

(134) (DT = C's apartment)
   M: Et puis il y a une partie cuisine, *moi* qui m'a émerveillée, tu vois. (I,4,15)
(135) *Moi*, l'incrustation me déplaît pas. (I,61,22)

Inanimate non-subject LDs, as in (136), tend also to be interpretable as the thing about which the accompanying clause expresses a property.

(136) et puis alors le *couscous*, on supporte pas de savoir qu'il *en* reste (II,43,20)

The application of this same notion of topic to cases of LD with no anaphor is often problematic, at least without some weakening of the semantic condition. The examples of (137) are representative of cases where the accompanying clause cannot be described as expressing a property of the initial Pro/NP.

(137) moi je sais que *cent deux*, mais je souffre [*cent deux* = number of second-quarter French course] (I,47,6)

(138) (DT = M's job of caretaker for an apartment building.)
    E: Est-ce que c'est très ennuyeux pour vous? Est-ce que vous avez souvent des problèmes avec les gens?
    M: Oh ben, y a des jours où comme tu sais *la fameuse tempête, le blizzard*, puisque j'ai vu dans l'dictionnaire qu'on disait blizzard en français aussi, *la fameuse tempête*, euh, pendant cinq heures, j'ai dû déblayer la neige toute seule [...] (I,4,22-23)

(139) *Moi*, notre, notre euh, ménagère euh, enfin pour le mariage a, a des poinçons. (III,12,4)

(140) *Moi*, le le le luthérianisme, le luthérianisme, de ma connaissance, c'est libéral. (I,71,8)

In fact, some examples which include an anaphor should be treated together with these cases, inasmuch as the anaphor is not topical, or is less topical than another NP/Pro in the clause, as in the examples of (141) and (142):

(141) mais *moi* il tombait toujours à mes pieds (*il* = the shotput) (II,33,24)

(142) *Moi*, c'est pas la personne qui me surprendrait le plus. [ç' = a previously mentioned NP] (III,67,17)

The preceding cases correspond rather well to Chafe's (1976: 50) description of Chinese-style topics, taken to be characteristic of topic-prominent languages. Rather than indicating 'what the sentence is about', this type of topic "sets a spatial, temporal, or individual framework within which the main predication holds." Given the rather overwhelming predominance in French of the subject-type topics, the question arises, is there some special motivation or explanation for the existence within French of these constructions which are apparently more typical of topic-prominent languages? The answer to this question lies in the special pragmatic functions of these constructions.

The no-anaphor LDs of the corpus form two sub-groups with slightly different pragmatic functions. These two sub-types correspond for the most part, but not entirely, to the distinction between pronominal and lexical NP detachments. The first type, which is largely restricted to NP detachments, is precisely the type of construction which Chafe describes as not ordinarily available in English (I am sure their status is the same in English and French), i.e., the topic NP is interpreted adverbially, giving the appearance of a PP from which the preposition has been deleted. For example:

(143) *1101*, il y a quand même plus de, de, de temps pour parler de ces choses-là. [1101 = course number of Beginning French] (I,47,6)

(144) Oh oeuh, mais tu sais, *l'métro*, avec la Carte Orange, tu vas n'importe où (II,79,18)

(145) parce que *les choux à la crème*, euh, i'faut qu'la crème refroidisse (I,46,19)

(146) *le restaurant que j'ouvrirai* donc, le jour où j'm'lancerai là-d'dans, y aura que'que chose 'Sorayia'. (I,41,12)

Such cases as these are attributable, I believe, to the spontaneous nature of the discourse in which they occur. That is, one of the well-known differences between planned and unplanned discourse is that the latter shows a lesser reliance on syntax to indicate relations between elements of an utterance, or between utterances. In other words, pragmatic linking takes the place of formal integration. (cf. Keenan and Schieffelin 1976: 255; Keenan 1977.)

The second type of no-anaphor LD may occur with either NP or Pro-detachments, though the latter, especially in the first person, are considerably more frequent. Larsson's (1979: 44) description of this construction-type is very similar to Keenan and Schieffelin's (1976: 244) description of the English LD function of pointing out a particular case of a general phenomenon under discussion. A slight variation on this is the alternative referent function, i.e. bringing in a different referent from one previously specified with respect to some predication (244). Both of these functions are performed by this type of no-anaphor LD. For example, (147) illustrates the pointing out of a particular case of a general phenomenon previously expressed:

(147) tu sais que les animaux, quand ils sentent qu'i' vont être euh, qu'y a le, l'oiseau de proie ou quoi que ce soit qui vient, qui les prend pour les manger, ils ont une certaine défense quoi, plus ou moins. Alors y en a, *le putois*, il y a l'odeur, etc. (I,19,18)

The more typical case corresponds to the alternative referent function; here, the accompanying clause usually begins with *c'est*, with the reference of *c'* typically being determined by one of two possible modes of interpretation. Representative of the first type of interpretation is the very frequent expression *moi c'est pareil*, as in (148):

(148) (DT = the annoying noise produced by housemates' musical endeavors)

> C: Et encore, tu sais, moi j'ai d'la chance, encore j'ai d'la chance parce que il fait, il fait un sacré effort pour pas, pour pas s'entraîner quand j'suis là, hein.
> E: Ben oui, mais tu sais, euh, c'est pas, oui ben *moi* c'est pareil.
> (I,8,1-2)

Note that the referent of *c'* in *c'est pareil* is not *moi*, as the meaning is not '*I* am the same'. Rather, *c'* has an impersonal interpretation (like that of *ça* in the expression *ça va*) equivalent roughly to 'the situation'. The corresponding expression of dissimilarity is also frequent, as in example (16):

> (149) B: Il me faut toujours une recette.
> C: *Moi* c'est l'contraire. (I,35,15-16)

The second type of interpretation of *c'* occurs in a very frequent utterance-type which represents a variation of Keenan and Schieffelin's 'alternative referent' function. In this case, not only does the initial NP/Pro represent an alternative referent, but the accompanying clause presents a related but alternative predication (at least one of the elements of the predication — predicate or argument — is changed). In other words, both this utterance and the preceding related one may be seen as presenting particular cases of a general phenomenon which is implied but not expressed. Consider (150):

> (150) M: Moi ça me manque, les P'tits Suisses, ça me manque. En France j'en mangeais tous les jours.
> C: Oh *moi*, c'est les yaourts. (I,25,4-5)

Here, the interpretation of *c'* depends crucially on the preceding discourse. In this case, one could say that *c'* derives its reference from the implicit discourse-topic, i.e. foods of France that the speakers miss while in this country. The presence of the initial *moi*, limiting the scope of the predication to the current speaker, results in the interpretation of *c'* as that thing which is missed by the current speaker. (151) presents a similar example:

> (151) (C. has just recounted an incident in her childhood where her mother insisted that she eat a blood sausage that she disliked.)
> E: Il fallait finir, hein. Il fallait finir. Moi j'étais (?).
> M: Et puis pas d'dessert si tu finis pas, hein.
> C: Exactement, moi aussi, il fallait finir.
> E: *Moi*, j'me rappelle, c'est la soupe. J'avais horreur d'la soupe.
> (II,66,7-10)

As in the previous example, the interpretation of *c'* results from the combination of the initial scope-setting *moi* with the current discourse-topic, things the speakers didn't like to eat as children.[45]

As mentioned above, the latter types of no-anaphor LDs (illustrated in (147)-(151) and supplying a particular case or an alternative referent) are much less common with lexical NPs than with pronominal detachments. Some examples corresponding to the type illustrated in (148) and (149) are given in (152) and (153):

(152) moi j'me suis dit, ça, des cacahuettes, j'adore ça, t'vois, j'suis une fanatique d'la cacahuète, vraiment, et *ma mère*, c'est pareil (II,48,15)

(153) Moi j'peux p-, vraiment tu vois, alors *le ketchup*, c'est pareil, j'peux pas manger ça. (II,48,12)

The *moi*-LD, however, possesses the possibility of an extremely indirect relation between the LD and the accompanying clause, to a degree which is impossible with NPs. For example, the discourse segment given in (154) occurs in a discussion about the speakers' introduction of cultural information in their French classes.

(154) M: Non, en tous les cas je leur avais dit, donc présenté toutes, toutes ces petites choses et ils adorent, ils adorent ça. Et cette année, donc, oh, cette année, ce quarter (?) quand je leur ai parlé euh, de l'Algérie, des évènements enfin plus ou moins, ils m'ont dit, mais pourquoi y a pas plus de, de de notes culturelles, évidemment.
E: Ah oui. *Moi* aussi, ils adorent ça. (I,50,7-8)

Here, the initial *moi* defines the framework for the following predication as E's experience or situation, with the result that the following *ils* is interpreted as referring to students in her class. In (155), the relation between *moi* and the predication is even more indirect, with *moi*, given the current discourse-topic, coming to be interpreted as 'in my class':

(155) (DT = silly answers their students have given to multiple-choice cultural questions on tests)
M: Moi je m'souviens, dans la, dans le, tu sais Jean-Paul Sartre est un, est célèbre pour: un, ses films, deux, ses chansons, trois, ses livres, et puis le quatrième, j'sais plus quoi. Mais j'en ai pas mal qui m'ont mis qu'il était célèbre pour ses chansons.

E: *Moi*, l'Italie est au milieu d'la France de temps en temps.
(II,27,3)

Note that in all the foregoing cases, the interpretation of the utterance depends on the drawing of a pragmatic link between the initial *moi* and the accompanying clause, and that the particular content of this link usually depends on the preceding discourse. A slightly different case is represented by (140) above. Here there is nothing in the clause which depends on the preceding discourse for its interpretation, and nothing in the prior discourse limits the scope of the prediction. Thus, the initial *moi* receives the maximally general interpretation of 'in my opinion'.

In conclusion, the range of possible interpretations of lefthand *moi* is clearly much broader than that of lefthand NPs, even where the latter have no anaphor in the clause. In some cases, lefthand *moi* does not satisfy Reinhart's definition of sentence-topic, but rather is reduced to the function of indicating the domain in which the following predication holds. This extension and concomitant weakening of the function of *moi* is of course related to the privileged status of the referent of *moi* as the initiator of the speech act, but it is also no doubt facilitated by the pervasiveness of *moi* in its topic-shifting function. Finally, I believe that the *moi*-no anaphor construction should be seen, like the NP-no anaphor type, as a feature of unplanned discourse, which allows considerable syntactic simplification, as shown, for example, by the frequent use of *c'est*. We have seen how this syntactic simplification is possible through reliance on pragmatic linking which usually depends crucially on knowledge of the preceding discourse.

6.3. Double LDs

The various treatments of LD in French generally touch upon the possibility of multiple LDs accompanying the same clause. For instance, Lambrecht (1981: 55, 73) notes that there may be a maximum of two LDs in a sentence and that their order is free, while Larsson (1979) considers and rejects the hypothesis that there is a hierarchical relation between multiple LDs.[46] The kind of double LD most often considered in the literature is that where each LD (usually each a lexical NP) has an anaphor in the clause, e.g.:

(156) Jean, des livres, je sais bien qu'elle lui en a volé beaucoup
(Hirschbühler 1975: 164)
(157) Mes parents, la liberté sexuelle et tout ça, ils en ont horreur.
(*Elle*, Larsson 1979: 15)

Lambrecht (1981) departs from this pattern somewhat: his examples have *moi* as one of the LD-expressions, and he also notes the existence of the 'double-subject' construction, i.e. where the first NP is selectionally unrelated to the verb, and the second includes a possessive marker referring to the first NP, as in (158) (Lambrecht 1981: 57):

(158) Mon frère, sa voiture el-est complètement cassée.

Hirschbühler also mentions the possibility of a lefthand NP being anaphorically related to a pronoun contained in another lefthand NP, as in (159) (Hirschbühler 1975: 164):

(159) Des livres, celui qui en a le plus, je crois qu'il s'appelle Pierre.

If we look at the cases of multiple LDs in this corpus, we find a noticeable discrepancy between the actual facts of spoken French and the picture of these constructions which is suggested by the foregoing literature. There are forty such constructions in all. Of these, only one has LD expressions which are both lexical NPs and which both have anaphors in the clause, as in (156) and (157) above:

(160) *le prof*, (euh) *même l'analyse*, il nous l'avait donnée   (II,40,21)

Note that (160) differs from (156) and (157) in that the second NP of (160) represents part of the new information of the utterance. In fact, it is no doubt the special nature of the pragmatic context required for both NPs to be recoverable which accounts for the relative rarity of this type of double LD.

Before going on to consider the predominant types of multiple LDs, I should note that there is a group of seven tokens which should probably be excluded from consideration, on the basis that the two LD-expressions are coreferent, one of them (either the first or the second) being the demonstrative pronoun *ça*, e.g.:

(161) *Oignon, ça* c'est l'exception.   (II,68,13)
(162) Et ben *ça, le bout*, il est bien?   (I,67,16)

More interesting are the cases of disreferent expressions. What distinguishes all of the remaining cases from the examples of (156) and (157) is either one or, more often, both of the following properties: (i) one of the LD-expressions is a first-person pronoun; (ii) only one of the expressions has an anaphor in the clause. In fact, thirty of the tokens have *moi* or *nous* as one of the LDs. Further subcategorization of these tokens according to whether *moi/nous* is the first or second expression reveals some interesting patterns.

We will consider first those cases where *moi/nous* is the second of the two detached expressions. Several of these have *ça* as the first expression. *Ça* may have an anaphor in the clause, e.g.:

(163) [...] *ça, moi* j'ai rien à dire là-d'dans   (III,18,15)

but it usually does not, e.g.:

(164) (C. has just told a story of how, as a child, her mother made her eat something she disliked)
E: *Ca, nous* c'était pareil.   (II,66,4)

In (164) and similar cases, the use of *ça* approaches the autonomous exclamatory use of this pronoun which is common in the spoken language, but it still qualifies here as a detached expression. Cases where the first expression is a lexical NP are similar to the preceding cases in that the NP usually represents the DT, and the utterance expresses the attitude or experience of the speaker in relation to that topic. While *moi* usually has an anaphor in the clause, this is not obligatory:

(165) Oui mais *le sauna*, alors *moi* j'aime pas tellement [...]   (II,7,20)
(166) Alors là, *la roue, moi* ça s'est très mal passé.   (II,35,14)

Examples such as (165) and (166) might lead one to ask if there is not a hierarchical relation between the two LD-expressions, inasmuch as the first refers to the more general DT and the second to the speaker. However, that this is not in fact a fixed order is indicated by (167), where the two LD-expressions occur in the reverse order but appear to function in essentially the same way as above:

(167) *Moi la gale*, c'était une histoire.   (III,61,11)

There is a slight pragmatic difference which may be significant, namely, *la gale* here refers to an earlier DT, this utterance coming just at the end of an intervening and related segment on lice. Thus, in (167), the NP-LD does not refer to the current DT. Nevertheless, the two LD-expressions in (165)-(167) seem to be interchangeable without any significant consequences. This is not the case for the majority of the double LDs where *moi/nous* is the first element. We turn to these now.

Of the twenty cases of this type, there are only two where the initial pronoun has an anaphor in the clause:

(168) et puis *moi, c'qu'y a*, c'est qu'j'aime pas [...]   (II,82,13)
(169) (DT = sofas)

Nous le nôtre, qui est affreux du reste, on l'avait eu [...]   (I,1,4)

The predominant type in this category has as the second LD-expression a *ce qu-* relative which is the antecedent of *ce* (*c'*) in the accompanying clause. In most cases, the *ce qu-* relative contains a first-person pronoun coreferent with the first LD-expression, so these are comparable to (159) above. The following are representative:

(170) *Moi*, le, quand j'étais à New York, *ce qui m'a surpris*, c'est les graffiti dans l'métro   (II,74,16)
(171) *Moi, c'que j'sais faire*, c'est l'saut en extension.   (II,35,15)

The initial *moi* may of course have no anaphor in either the relative or the accompanying clause:

(172) *Moi, c'qui était amusant*, c'est mon frère a eu, (il) est allergique à la, pénicilline.   (III,54,20)

(173) is similar, but with an ordinary NP rather than a relative as the second LD-expression:

(173) *Moi, le le le luthérianisme, le luthérianisme*, de ma connaissance, c'est libéral.   (I,71,8)

Notice that in (170)-(173), the order of the two LD-expressions cannot be reversed without making the utterance pragmatically bizarre. It may appear, in (170) and (171), that this is due to the fact that the clitics *me* and *je* would then precede *moi*, but the similarity of the result in (172) and (173) suggests a more general explanation. The principle which seems to be at work is that where one of the two LD-expressions is only rather loosely linked (semantically or pragmatically) to the following predication, that expression must come before the one which is more closely related to the predication. In other words, I am suggesting that the kind of topic hierarchy considered by Larsson (1979: 16), where the first expression refers to a more general topic and sets the limits within which the second expression is to be interpreted, does apply just in case there is a significant difference between the two expressions in the degree to which they are related to the predication. That the most frequent realization of this kind of case is with *moi/nous* as the less closely linked expression is simply a reflection of the observations made in sec. 6.2 concerning the extension of the pragmatic functions of lefhand *moi/nous* beyond the usual functions of LD with other pronouns or NPs.

Notice that I have not equated a closer link between a detached expression and the accompanying predication with the occurrence of an anaphor in the clause. Example (166) above shows that a close pragmatic link does not depend on the presence of an anaphor in the clause. (166) and (167) are comparable in that in each case the NP-LD has an anaphor in the clause while *moi* does not. However, it is clear in both cases that the predication is describing an experience of the speaker's in relation to the NP topic. Thus, I would claim that the reasons why the order of the LD-expressions is not fixed is that both of the expressions are closely related to the predication. What is different about (172) and (173) is that here the information given by the predication does not pertain primarily to an experience of the speaker's. An additional illustration of the nonnecessity of a correlation between the presence or absence of an anaphor and the degree of relatedness to the predication is furnished by the third instance of LD in example (16) in sec. 3.2.1 above (Alors *nous, les cafés*, bon, un café). In this case, though neither of the LD-expressions has an anaphor in the (elliptical) clause, it is clear that *les cafés* is more closely related to what follows. As expected, permutation of the LD-expressions makes the utterance pragmatically unacceptable.

A few illustrations of this principle can be found with expressions other than *moi/nous* as the first LD. I think that (164) above is one such case. Again, neither LD-expression has an anaphor in the clause, but the initial *ça*, referring to the situation just described by C., is less directly related than *nous* to the following predication. The following shows a similar use of *ça*:

(174) (Speakers are discussing the various athletic activities in their *lycée* experiences.)
M: Et la corde?
C: Oh la corde! J'ai jamais su monter.
M: Alors *ça, ceux qui étaient trop lourdauds, ceux qu(i) étaient trop lourdauds*, on les, on mettait une corde avec des noeuds pour eux. (II,37,7)

Again, note that the permutation of the LD-expressions in both (164) and (174) produces an unacceptable utterance. There is one example illustrating this principle where the initial expression is a lexical NP:

(175) *La clarinette*, si tu veux, *ce qu'y a de merveilleux dans cet instrument*, c'est, ça a une pureté de son (I,60,7)

The 'double-subject' construction illustrated by Lambrecht's example given in (158) above is of course another particular case of the principle proposed above, in that the 'possessor' is always less directly involved in the predication than the 'thing possessed'. This corpus yielded five examples which I think are comparable to (158), but note that all five of them are with *moi/nous* as the initial LD-expression; moreover, contrary to Lambrecht's indication, in two tokens the NP denoting the thing possessed has the definite rather than the possessive determiner.

(176) *Moi mon père*, il est terrible (II,43,9)
(177) *Nous la chambre d'invités*, c'est la chambre où il y a le bureau. (I,7,7)
(177) [...] le mobilier, tu sais dans la famille, *nous le mobilier*, c'est tout le mobilier que ma mère a [...] (I,56,16)

The omission of an overt possessive marker seems to depend both on the nature of the referent of the second NP (cf. *??moi, le père, il est terrible*) and on the nature of the first LD-expression (cf. *??Jacques, la chambre d'invités, c'est la chambre* [...]). On this and the more general question addressed above, our conclusions must of course remain somewhat tentative, given the limited data on which they are based. Given what I consider to be the infeasibility of obtaining valid speaker-intuitions on pragmatic aspects of utterances which may occur in actual spoken discourse, I think a more definite answer to these questions lies in the examination of more corpuses of actual oral discourse.

7. CONCLUSION

Through a detailed examination of the various types of LD occurring in the corpus, we have arrived at a more nuanced description of the pragmatic function of LD than the previously prevailing view of LD as overtly marking the topic-comment relation and effecting a shift in the DT. We have observed a certain diversity of specific functions, along with a basic unity of functions at a more general level. While it is true that virtually all LD-expressions represent the sentence-topic, it is only in one case that this relation is sufficient to motivate the LD. This is the special case of the NP *c'est* LD, whose nearly grammaticalized status was seen as related to the identificational function of *c'est*, NP *c'est* ... being the expression of what one might call the topic-comment relation 'par excellence'. In most other cases, the LD-referent is not only the sentence-topic but is also topical in the discourse.

Other cases of LD where the LD-referent is not a DT have been attributed to various specific motivations. One such case involves the preposing of an NP of the type described as having no discourse referent (e.g. *c'qu'y a*, *c'est que* ...), which serves either to introduce a proposition or infinitive, or to allow what is presupposed to precede new information. Other more minor cases have to do with the introduction (within foregrounded discourse) of an NP whose referent is not 'motivated' by the preceding discourse or the extralinguistic context, and with the presence of hesitation particles after the NP. While the sentential topic-comment relation is not sufficient motivation for most cases of LD, it is nevertheless this articulation of the utterance into a preposed topic portion and a following comment portion which constitutes the basic pragmatic function which is common to *all* instances of LD.

The present data confirm Larsson's observation that the LD-referent is not necessarily 'given', but rather is simply 'motivated'. We have seen various particular ways in which the LD-referent may be 'motivated' by the preceding context. In fact, a slight qualification must be added to Larsson's statement concerning the 'motivation' of the referent since, as we have seen, there are some cases where the LD-referent itself is in no way motivated by the preceding context or the situation. In such cases, however, cohesion is always assured by other cohesive links. This was seen to be an important difference between LD and the presentational *ya* construction, as only the latter may occur in the absence of any cohesive links with the preceding context.

The evidence of this corpus forces us to discard the old notion that LD-referents differ from the referents of lexical subjects in being more constrained with respect to 'givenness' or prior knowledge. The only constraint of this type is that LD-referents cannot be 'Brand-New' (i.e. not already identifiable by the hearer), and it was noted that this constraint characterizes subjects as well in spoken French. What does appear to be an accurate predictor of the occurrence of LD vs. a lexical subject is the grounding principle which Lambrecht (1984a,b) borrows from Hopper (1979) and proposes to use for this purpose. While the principle proposed by Lambrecht is roughly equivalent to the claim that LD-referents are DTs while lexical subjects are not, we saw that certain cases require a more precise statement allowing for the independence of grounding (i.e. foreground vs. background status of the discourse segment) and discourse-topicality. In addition, various problems were noted in the application to conversation of a principle originally proposed for narrative discourse. On the whole, however, the correlation of LD and foregrounded discourse or discourse-topicality is confirmed by the present data, taking into account the various 'exceptions' noted above. Moreover, the operation of the principle was observed not only with lexical NP detachments but also with pronominal (*moi*) LDs.

It seems to me that the fact that LD is largely limited to foregrounded discourse is a particularly cogent argument against the view of LD as primarily a syntactic phenomenon (i.e. which sees the LD-anaphor as a new subject agreement marker). Moreover, the existence of a significant group of LDs of no or minimal pragmatic motivation which such a view predicts, is clearly discomfirmed by the data. The most likely candidates for such 'unmotivated' cases would be the NP *c'est* LDs, as these are not always pragmatically motivated at the level of the discourse. However, the very fact that such cases are largely limited to the NP *c'est* type suggests that some other motivation (at the sentence level) is involved, as has been suggested above.

The fact that the overwhelming majority of the LD occurrences are clearly pragmatically motivated, together with the fundamental pragmatic unity of the various types of LDs, also refutes the hypothesis that two basic types of LDs may be distinguished according to the presence or absence of pragmatic motivation. A related issue is the question of how the pragmatics of LD in French compares to that of English LDs. As a corrollary to his syntactic-pragmatic correlation hypothesis (cf. sec. 2.1), Cinque (1977: 41) suggests that languages differ in that some, such as French, have both types, i.e. with and without clear pragmatic motivation, while other languages, such as English, have only the pragmatically motivated type. I would argue rather that at least in its discourse-level functions, LD in French is pragmatically very similar to LD in English. I believe we have seen that Keenan and Schieffelin's (1976: 242) description of the primary function of LD in English applies just as well to LD in French, namely, to bring into the foreground of the listener's consciousness a referent which is usually not currently a 'center of attention'. We have repeatedly made reference to Keenan and Schieffelin's 'alternative referent' and 'particular case' functions as more specific descriptions of many of the examples from this corpus.

It does appear, however, that there are differences in the two languages with respect to the relative frequency of pragmatic subtypes according to the information status of the LD-referent. Though confirmation of this hypothesis requires more precise information than what is furnished by Keenan and Schieffelin, it appears that the typical LD-referent in French is already (before the LD) more prominent in the listener's consciousness than is the case in the typical English LD. While the present French data reveal that the LD-referent need not be 'given' and is in fact new to the discourse in a significant number of cases, the more frequent case in French is that where the LD-referent has been mentioned in the very recent discourse. Keenan and Schieffelin (1976: 242), on the other hand, appear to suggest that the introduction of discourse-new referents is the most common function of LD in English. While they point out that some LD-referents do appear in the preceding discourse, these cases seem somewhat different from the typical French case in that, in English, the referent has already "fallen into the background" following its first mention. Another indication of the fact that LD in French typically involves referents which are relatively more foregrounded to start with, is the high frequency of *moi*-LDs compared to the rare occurrence of first- or second-person LD-referents in English, explained by Keenan and Schieffelin (1976: 246) as "due to their near constant presence in the discourse history". This pragmatic difference between the two languages would also account for the apparent higher frequency of LD in spoken French than in spoken English.

Thus, I believe it is clear that LD performs the same basic function, as well as largely the same set of specific functions in French and English, but the most typical case in each language differs with respect to the previous information status of the LD-referent. I believe this difference finds its explanation in Lambrecht's (1984a,b) constraint on subjects in spoken French, to the effect that, in foregrounded discourse, a grammatical subject must be not only the sentence-topic but also already given or the center of attention (i.e. in syntactic terms, it will always be pronominal). It is ultimately the application of this constraint to spoken French but not to spoken English that accounts for the greater use of LD in French than in English.

The foregoing furnishes two additional arguments for the view of LD in French as primarily not a syntactic phenomenon characteristic of a certain language variety, but rather as a pragmatic phenomenon occurring in spontaneous speech:

(a) The fundamental similarity of French LDs to English LDs, together with Keenan and Schieffelin's (1976) conclusion that the latter represent a form of unplanned speech.

(b) The essentially pragmatic nature of the givenness constraint on subjects which occasions the use of LD. Lambrecht (1984a,b) furnishes substantial evidence that this constraint is pragmatic rather than syntactic in nature.

The claim that LD is primarily a feature of unplanned oral discourse predicts that LD ought to occur with approximately equal relative frequency in the speech of speakers of varying socio-economic standing. Confirmation of this prediction requires careful comparison of corpuses such as this one and others where the variety of French is further removed from the standard language.

As a final note, I would like to point out that the grounding principle (viz. that the givenness constraint on subjects applies only in foregrounded parts of a discourse) in fact suggests that, at least for French, LD is a feature not of spoken language, or even of spontaneous spoken language, but rather of a certain subset of spontaneous spoken language, namely the foregrounded parts. In other words, it appears that, in the backgrounded parts of a discourse, *on parle comme un livre*, or at least, that those parts of the discourse are in some respects more like written or planned language than the foregrounded parts. Whether this is true, and why it should be so, are subjects for future research.

NOTES

1. The question of where to draw the line between Standard and Nonstandard French is somewhat problematic, due to the interaction of social class distinctions and differences of medium (spoken/written) and of register (formal/informal). By 'informal spoken Standard French', I mean the language spoken by educated speakers in an informal situation. Lambrecht (1981) cuts the pie differently, preferring to use the term NonStandard French for the spoken language, inasmuch as the notion of Standard French has always been strongly associated with the written language. (Cf. Lambrecht 1981: 13-14.)

2. See Lambrecht (1981: 8-10) for a summary of some of these observations.

3. Keenan (1977) describes left detachment (LD) constructions in English (with or without an anaphor in the clause) as characteristic of spontaneous conversation. Duranti and Ochs (1979) do the same for LD in Italian.

4. Lambrecht's list includes in addition a few other features concerning use of pronouns. For the most part, these seem not to occur in the corpus due simply to the nonoccurrence of the necessary context.

5. The speech sample studied here consists of three audio recordings of approximately two hours each of the same group of three native speakers plus this researcher, engaged in spontaneous conversation. The participants were graduate students in French literature employed as teaching assistants and who already knew each other well. Recordings were made in my home, to ensure an informal atmosphere. Though I at times participated in the conversation, I made no attempt to direct the conversation in any way. (My interventions have of course not been considered for purposes of the study.) All participants happened to be female, and were between the ages of 21 and 27. Speakers E and M come from upper middle class families, while C describes hers as working class. The subjects varied in length of previous residence in this country from about two years to four months. This was not believed to be an important factor for this study.

6. e.g. the Coordinate Structure Constraint, Complex NP Constraint, Sentential Subject Constraint (cf. Ross 1967). For illustration of their application to these structures, see Hirschbühler (1975), Cinque (1977), or Larsson (1979: 118-120).

7. According to Larsson (1979), French shows a comparable phenomenon in the possible occurrence in the LD-expression of a 'déterminant réfléchi', i.e. a third-person possessive determiner coreferent with a NP in the following clause, e.g. (Larsson's (27), p. 116)):

(i) Son$_i$ (propre) enfant, elle$_i$ l'adore, cette mère.

In my opinion, however, given the semantic nature of this relation (as noted by Larsson), it would be better handled by independently necessary interpretive rules of coreference, rather than by transformational derivation. That this approach would be preferable is indicated by a problematic example pointed out by Larsson herself (her example (79), p. 125):

(ii) ?Sa$_i$ femme, Pierre$_i$ adore cette idiote.

According to Larsson's analysis, this sentence ought to be excluded since the presence of the possessive determiner in the LD supposedly requires a transformational origin, while the NP anaphor requires base generation.

8. This feature is not specifically mentioned by Cinque, but is included in the interest of completeness.

9. Examples (7) and (8) are Larsson's (59) and (60), p. 122.

10. The terms 'old information' and 'new information' are open to any number of various interpretations. The sense Cinque apparently intends is that a left-dislocated NP must already be a topic of the discourse, whereas the referent of a Hanging Topic was not previously a topic. Information statuses of LD-referents are discussed at length in sec. 5.2.

11. This is borne out by certain examples from the corpus of LDs whose referents are new to the discourse; see sec. 5.2.2.

12. A few remarks on the transcription are in order. First, note that the speaker referred to as 'B' is myself (a nonnative speaker). Where the transcription is uncertain, either the possible transcription or a question mark is enclosed in parentheses. Unless otherwise indicated, overlapping turns are indicated by a vertical line in the lefthand margin. A hyphen indicates partial words. References in parentheses following each citation refer to its location in the corpus (number of the recording session, page, and turn(s)). The transcription used is strictly orthographic and uses conventional punctuation, though commas are usually omitted following LDs, except in the case of a perceivable pause. Though typical phonological features of the spoken language are sometimes indicated (e.g. *p'tit*, *i'vient*), the transcription should not be taken as strictly accurate in these respects. Single underlining is used simply to highlight detached expressions and (in the case of lexical LDs) their anaphors, while double underlining indicates extra stress.

13. I am referring here to certain well-established constraints such as the nonoccurrence of LD in subordinate nonasserted clauses, with referentially indefinite referents, with quantified NPs, or with unrestricted indefinite pronouns (e.g. *tout le monde*). Cf. Larsson (1979: 29-31), Lambrecht (1984b: 25, 27-28).

14. Some would argue that the detached NP of (21) is not 'new' because it is inferrable; I argue the opposing point of view in sec. 5.2.2 below, where information statuses of LD-referents are discussed at length. It may be, however, that drawing finer distinctions in degree of 'newness', or degree of 'motivation' (cf. sec. 5.2.1), will confirm a corrrelation between high pitch and 'unexpectedness' or lack of 'motivation'.

15. There is a very small group of examples which suggest the existence of an alternative descending intonation contour. However, some of these cases should no doubt be considered to be two separate utterances rather than a LD construction, as in the following (note the pause following the NP):

> enfin, je l'ai quand même appelé au téléphone et je lui ai dit, enfin J., *cette fille* / elle est vraiment vierge? (III,73,9)

One clear example of a LD construction with a slightly descending intonation contour is the following (M. has been talking about how poorly she usually did in her history-geography class, and then describes that part of her baccalaureat exam):

> M: [...] J'ai eu, j'ai eu 16 ou 18, enfin pas possible, une des meilleures notes de tout le groupe. Le prof, il en pouvait plus enfin.
>
> C: *Ton père*, il en pouvait plus. (II,40,22)

(The final rising intonation seems to indicate continuation, rather than an interrogative.)

16. There are just a handful of other cases which may be problematic, namely LDs in clauses which are either syntactically or pragmatically subordinate. These would pose a problem if these clauses cannot be said to be asserted, and if, in fact, assertion is held to be a necessary condition for the topic-comment relation. Given the thorny nature of the question of subordination and assertion, I will not deal with these questions here. Some examples of this type are given in 3.4 above.

17. Duranti and Ochs (1979: 391) note that evidence from Italian suggests the need for a further distinction between speaker and addressee. That is (using the language of the present discussion), the quasi-constraint requiring the use of a detached pronoun when the speaker is not already topical is not as strong for the second person. Duranti and Ochs found in their Italian corpus that nearly half of the second-person subject-verb agreement referents (i.e. without LD) occurred where the addressee referent did not occur in the immediately preceding discourse. I am certain the same holds true for French as well. Of the ten instances of *toi*-LDs in the corpus, all are clearly comparative or emphatic, or generic in interpretation. Duranti and Ochs suggest an explanation based on the egocentric nature of attention: "[...] speakers may assume that the addressee has been attending to himself even if there has not been talk about himself. The speaker does not assume, however, that the addressee has been attending to the current speaker."

18. Unlike most of her peers, M. always addresses me, in all situations, with the formal *vous*.

19. Cf. Lambrecht (1981: 19-20) for discussion of the double function of *ça* as an independent pronoun and as a clitic.

20. Included in this group are 23 instances with other tense forms of *être*: *c'était* (16), *ce sont* (3), *c'était/c'étaient* (2), *ce sera* (1), *ce serait* (1).

21. The distinction in referential properties between *ce/c'* and *il(s)/elle(s)* is parallelled by an exactly comparable distinction between the dative clitics *lui/leur* and adverbial clitic *y*. Cf. Barnes (1980).

22. Of course, the grammatical neutrality of *c'est* is reflected in the standard written language with respect to gender, its adjective complement being always in the neuter, or masculine singular form.

23. An interesting anomaly sometimes occurs in comparable English constructions. These are among several examples I have heard:

(i)　　　The point **is**, is that [...]
(ii)　　　The weird thing about it is, is that the hospital census is quite low.
(iii)　　What their goal is, is to reduce [...]

The first occurrence of *is* is often stressed (especially where the preceding NP is relatively short) and is followed by a slight pause. Also note the quasi-adverbial use of the expressioon *trouble is*, e.g. as in (iv):

(iv)　　Trouble is, I can't get anyone to go with me.

24. While (69c) is grammatical in Standard French, it is in fact the case, as pointed out by Lambrecht (1984a, 1984b), that in spoken French, NPs which are referentially indefinite are excluded from subject position. Comparisons of the sort found in (69) were typically made with reference to the standard (i.e. written) language, rather than to actual spoken French.

25. 'Given' refers to a referent which may be assumed to be in the listener's consciousness at the time of the utterance (Chafe 1976: 30). As for 'evoked', a referent may be either textually or situationally evoked, that is, previously mentioned in the discourse, or a salient part of the situational context. An inferrable entity is one which the speaker assumes may be inferred by logical or plausible reasoning from entities already evoked or other inferrable entities. (Prince 1981a: 236)

26. This definition, strictly applied, could even include entities which may be salient in the situational context, but these seem to behave more like textually evoked referents.

27. I believe that Lambrecht is referring to the New-Unused category when he states (1984a: 5) that "there are [...] no examples found in corpuses of definite NPs in [LD] position whose referents are new in the narrow context of the utterance but identifiable by the addressee at the level of long-term memory". However, it is clear from other comments that Lambrecht allows an extremely broad notion of 'recoverable' and, consequently, an extremely narrow notion of 'new', so that the problem here may be a terminological one. (Cf. fn. 33 below.)

28. Since the more controversial category with respect to LD is that of New-Unused, I will make some observations below concerning this category alone. However, in the general exposition of the ways in which LD-referents are 'motivated', New-Unused and Inferrable will be treated as one category. I think this treatment is justified by the similarity of their behavior. Prince herself (1981a: 252) suggests the possibility of the appropriateness of collapsing these two categories.

29. Cf. sec. 5.1.1 above, and also Prince (1981a: 229-30) for some discussion of similar cases in English.

30. Lambrecht (1984b: 14) points this out and relates it to the topic-shifting function of LD vs. the topic continuity of right detachment.

31. Recall that a discourse-topic is an entity or proposition which a segment of discourse larger than a sentence is about; i.e. that stretch of discourse is understood as intending to expand the discourse participants' knowledge of that entity or proposition (cf. sec. 3.6).

32. Notice that this type of context furnishes strong supporting evidence for Lambrecht's claim that LD serves to promote a referent to the status of 'given' in order to satisfy the givenness constraint on subjects in spoken French (1984a, 1984b). Since the referents in question are already DTs, a description of LD as essentially (re)establishing a referent as a DT does not account for these cases.

33. The extremely broad sense in which Lambrecht uses *recoverable* is evident in his discussion of an example involving a 'frame of reference' referential link (1984a: 16). In reference to the following exchange between a husband and wife at dinner:

    H: Ca n'a pas de goût, ce poulet

    W: Le veau, c'est pire

Lambrecht states that "the referent of *le veau* is [...] recoverable because it takes part in the general 'meat scenario' that was evoked by the husband's remark about the chicken". I think that such a broad use of *recoverable* is problematic in that it blurs the distinction between the contribution of the referent itself (i.e. its information status) and that of other independent factors (i.e. set-membership, frame of reference relations, etc.) which effect cohesion.

34. As pointed out by Lambrecht (personal communication), it may in fact be the case that *George* in (103) should not be considered a LD but rather as a focus constituent of an ellipted

clause. This type of autonomous NP frequently occurs in interrogative contexts as in (103). I do not have a precise answer to the question of how to identify LDs, but generally have made use of the context and/or intonation. Generally, a descending intonation contour has been taken as indicating a non-LD (cf. fn. 15). The intonation contour of *George* in (103) is rising, like that of the typical NP-LD.

35. Of the many occurrences of the NP subject *la balle*, only the two underlined are cases where LD would be an alternative, since all the others are in nonasserted subordinate clauses. Moreover, in the first of these two cases, the possibility of LD as an alternative structure may be diminished by the fact that the NP, in a repair, appears to have been substituted for the pronoun *elle*, probably because of the potential ambiguity of *elle* between the antecedents *balle* and *personne*. However, this in no way weakens the present argument, which has to do simply with the occurrence of a nontopical referent in a foregrounded part of this discourse.

36. Note, however, that the passage describing the game is, from the point of view of syntactic form, more like narration than description, since it represents a series of actions. It is of course the timeless nature of these actions (and the nonspecific nature of the participants) which makes the passage descriptive in function. It may be that desciptions of games represent in themselves a very particular type of discourse.

37. Lambrecht (1984b: 26), in pointing out the low transitivity of the clauses in which lexical subject NPs occur, suggests that *dire* should in fact be considered intransitive.

38. I do not include here the very few cases of NP-LDs with nonclitic (i.e. nonsubject) *ça* as the anaphor. It is not clear whether these cases have the same status as LDs with clitic anaphors, and they are so few in number that they are of little importance.

39. The following example appears to present an exception to the foregoing principle in that the LD-referent is New-Unused, and the anaphor in the following clause is an indirect object:

> (DT = a particular case of M's palmreading activity)
>
> M: [...] Je lui dis exactement l'âge, il faut l'faire, ça aussi. Par example, *J.*, je lui ai dit sa première relation sexuelle, il en revenait pas, à quel âge, à quel âge il l'avait. (III,71,1)

One might argue that here the topicality of the LD-expression is assured by the fact that both the LD-referent and the accompanying proposition constitute a particular case of the general phenomenon just referred to (the fact that one must tell the person at what age the event happened/will happen). In fact, however, if we more closely examine the example, we find that the first clause following the LD is in fact interpretable as a subordinate clause with an unexpressed *quand* (final intonation is rising), so that the more important thing said about J. is how he reacted, which is of course expressed with the LD-anaphor in subject position.

40. Actually, the 'as for' phrase seems a bit more appropriate in (120) than in (121). Given that the LD of (120) is recalling an earlier DT, the utterance could be loosely paraphrased as: "going back to the subject of beet soup, I've had some before [...]". (121) appears to be rather different in that there is no prior mention of the LD-referent; it is possible, however, that it is situationally evoked, since the speakers are eating some fresh vegetables and dip, but it is difficult to assess whether these were a salient part of the situation, or whether this connection existed in the minds of the speaker or listeners. In fact, the LD of (121) seems to be functioning like an emphatic focus constituent, i.e. like English 'topicalized' "*Vegetables* we **had**".

It should be noted that, in the case of the indefinite anaphor *en*, as in (121), the determiner of the left-detached NP may be either definite or indefinite; that is, the following is to be compared to (121):

> *Les biscuits à la cuiller*, on (en) a jamais mangé en dehors de la maladie (III,50,11)

41. There seems to be some slight evidence that it is primarily the pragmatic, and not the syntactic status of the expression that is crucial. If we consider the nondetached versions of (120) and (121) (i.e. *j'ai déjà mangé une soupe à la betterave, on avait des légumes*), the specific interpretation is the only one possible if the utterance carries the unmarked intonation and stress pattern that marks these utterance-final constituents as new information. On the other hand, if the direct objects carry the low intonation of anaphoric material, it seems to me that the given expressions may bear the nonspecific interpretations, as in the detached versions. The latter rendering of course entails that the same referent occurs in the preceding discourse with a generic interpretation (or that members of the set denoted by the NP are topical in the prior discourse).

42. The no-anaphor constructions studied here are distinguished from those examined in sec. 6.2 by the fact that in the present constructions, the clause following the initial NP contains a clear 'gap' corresponding to the lefthand NP. (The constructions of this section are not included in the total given in Table 1 of sec. 3.1.)

43. Prince (1981b: 259) describes Focus Movement as follows: "The [initial] NP represents the value of an attribute and it is new in the discourse. The open sentence resulting from the replacement of that constituent by a variable conveys the information that some entity has some attribute and it represents salient/given information in the discourse."

44. The absence of an anaphor with the verb *employer*, without an occurrence of the antecedent immediately preceding the clause, gives credence to Lambrecht's suggestion (personal communication) that these zero morphemes stand for a gap in the clitic paradigm corresponding to the impossible preverbal direct object *ça*, the direct object clitic *le* being reserved for a different kind of referent. Perhaps this distinction between Ø (=*ça*) and *le* is similar to the distinction between *ce/ça* and *il(s)/elle(s)* described in sec. 5.1.1 (and between *y* and *lui/leur*; cf. Barnes 1980).

45. As Lambrecht has pointed out (personal communication), the LD utterances of (150) and (151) may be considered as cleft constructions in which the following predication (i.e. relative clause, e.g. *qui me manquent, que je devais finir*) is understood.

46. The following example could be cited as a counterexample to the two LD limit, but it is clear that this is a rather special case and quite different from the kind of case Lambrecht means to rule out: *Moi c'que j'dis, ce qui est plus impressionnant, c'est de mettre des petits jeunes comme nous, des débutants euh* [...] (III,36,21).

REFERENCES

Bally, C.
    1932/1965   *Linguistique générale et linguistique française*. Bern: Francke.

Barnes, B.K.
    1980   "The notion of 'dative' in linguistic theory and the grammar of French". *Lingvisticae Investigationes* 4.245-292.

Bauche, H.
    1928   *Le langage populaire*. Paris: Payot.

Brown, G. and G. Yule
    1983   *Discourse analysis*. Cambridge: Cambridge University Press.

Chafe, W.L.
    1976   "Givenness, contrastiveness, definiteness, subjects, topics and point of view". In C. Li (ed.), 27-55.

Cinque, G.
    1977   "The movement nature of Left Dislocation". *Linguistic Inquiry* 8.397-411.

Deulofeu, J.
    1979   "Les énoncés à constituant lexical détaché: Les limites de l'organisation grammaticale et de l'organisation discursive dans ces énoncés". *Recherches sur le français parlé* 1:2.75-109.

Dik, S.
    1978   *Functional grammar*. Amsterdam: North-Holland.

Dijk, T.A. van
    1977   *Text and context*. London: Longman.

Duranti, A. and E. Ochs
    1979   "Left dislocation in Italian conversation". In T. Givón (ed.), 377-416.

Galambos, S.J.
    1980   "A clarification of the notion of topic: Evidence from popular spoken French". In J. Kreiman and E.A. Ojeda (eds.), *Papers from the parasession on pronouns and anaphora*. Chicago: Chicago Linguistic Society, 125-138.

Givón, T. (ed.)
    1979   *Discourse and syntax*. (= Syntax and Semantics, 12.) New York: Academic Press.

Hankamer, J.
    1974   "On the non-cyclic nature of WH-clefting". *Chicago Linguistic Society* 10.221-233.

Hirschbühler, P.
    1975   "On the source of lefthand NPs in French". *Linguistic Inquiry* 6:1.155-165.

Hopper, P.J.
    1979   "Aspects and foregrounding in discourse". In T. Givón (ed.), 213-241.

Hopper, P.J.
and S.A. Thompson
    1980   "Transitivity in grammar and discourse". *Language* 56:2.251-299.

Karttunen, L.
    1976   "Discourse referents". In J. McCawley (ed.), *Notes from the linguistic underground*. (= Syntax and semantics, 7.) New York: Academic Press, 363-385.

Kayne, R.
    1975   *French syntax: The transformational cycle*. Cambridge, Massachusetts: M.I.T. Press.

Keenan Ochs, E.
    1977   "Why look at unplanned and planned discourse?" In E. Keenan Ochs and T.L. Bennett (eds), *Discourse across space and time*. Southern California Occasional Papers in Linguistics VI.

Keenan Ochs, E. and B. Schieffelin
    1976   "Foregrounding referents: A reconsideration of left dislocation in discourse". *Berkeley Linguistics Society* 2.240-257.

Labov, W.
    1972   *Sociolinguistic patterns*. Philadelphia: University of Pennsylvania Press.

Lambrecht, K.
    1980   "Topic, French Style: Remarks about a basic sentence type of Modern Non-Standard French". *Berkeley Linguistics Society* 6.337-360.

    1981   *Topic, antitopic and verb agreement in non-standard French*. (= Pragmatics and Beyond, II:6.) Amsterdam: John Benjamins.

    1984a   "A pragmatic constraint on lexical subjects in spoken French". To appear in *Chicago Linguistic Society* 20.

    1984b   "On the status of SVO sentences in French discourse". To appear in Russ Tomlin (ed.), *Coherence and Grounding in Discourse*. Amsterdam: John Benjamins.

Larsson, E.
    1979   *La dislocation en français: Etude de syntaxe générative*. (= Etudes romanes de Lund, 28.) Lund: CWK Gleerup.

Li, C.N. (ed.)
    1976   *Subject and topic*. New York: Academic Press.

REFERENCES

Li, C.N. and S.A. Thompson
    1976   "Subject and topic: A new typology of language". In C. Li (ed.), 457-489.

Prince, E.F.
    1978   "A comparison of *wh*-clefts and *it*-clefts in discourse". *Language* 54.883-906.

    1981a   "Toward a taxonomy of given-new information". In P. Cole (ed.), *Radical pragmatics*. New York: Academic Press, 223-255.

    1981b   "Topicalization, focus movement and Yiddish movement: A pragmatic differentiation". *Berkeley Linguistics Society* 7.249-264.

Reinhart, T.
    1982   "Pragmatics and linguistics: An analysis of sentence topics". Distributed by Indiana University Linguistics Club, Bloomington, Indiana.

Ross, J.R.
    1967   "Constraints on variables in syntax". Ph.D. Thesis, M.I.T. Distributed by Indiana University Linguistics Club.

Silva-Corvalan, C.
    1983   "On the interaction of word order and intonation: Some OV constructions in Spanish". In Flora-Klein Andreu (ed.), *Discourse perspectives on syntax*. New York: Academic Press, 117-140.

Wartburg, W. von
    1946   *Problèmes et méthodes de la linguistique*, translated by Pierre Maillard. Paris: Presses Universitaires de France.

In the PRAGMATICS & BEYOND series the following monographs have been published thus far:

I:1. *Anca M. Nemoianu*: The Boat's Gonna Leave: A Study of Children Learning a Second Language from Conversations with Other Children.
Amsterdam, 1980, vi, 116 pp. Paperbound.

I:2. *Michael D. Fortescue*: A Discourse Production Model for 'Twenty Questions'.
Amsterdam, 1980, x, 137 pp. Paperbound.

I:3. *Melvin Joseph Adler*: A Pragmatic Logic for Commands.
Amsterdam, 1980, viii, 131 pp. Paperbound.

I:4. *Jef Verschueren*: On Speech Act Verbs.
Amsterdam, 1980, viii, 83 pp. Paperbound.

I:5. *Geoffrey N. Leech*: Explorations in Semantics and Pragmatics.
Amsterdam, 1980, viii, 133 pp. Paperbound. Temporarily out of print.

I:6. *Herman Parret*: Contexts of Understanding.
Amsterdam, 1980, viii, 109 pp. Paperbound.

I:7. *Benoît de Cornulier*: Meaning Detachment.
Amsterdam, 1980, vi, 124 pp. Paperbound.

I:8. *Peter Eglin*: Talk and Taxonomy: A methodological comparison of ethnosemantics and ethnomethodology with reference to terms for Canadian doctors.
Amsterdam, 1980, x, 125 pp. Paperbound.

II:1. *John Dinsmore*: The Inheritance of Presupposition.
Amsterdam, 1981, vi, 97 pp. Paperbound.

II:2. *Charles Travis*: The True and the False: The Domain of the Pragmatic.
Amsterdam, 1981, vi, 164 pp. Paperbound.

II:3. *Johan Van der Auwera*: What do we talk about when we talk? Speculative grammar and the semantics and pragmatics of focus.
Amsterdam, 1981, vi, 121 pp. Paperbound.

II:4. *Joseph F. Kess & Ronald A. Hoppe*: Ambiguity in Psycholinguistics.
Amsterdam, 1981, v, 123 pp. Paperbound.

II:5. *Karl Sornig*: Lexical Innovation: A Study of Slang, Colloquialisms and Casual Speech.
Amsterdam, 1981, viii, 117 pp. Paperbound.

II:6. *Knud Lambrecht*: Topic, Antitopic and Verb Agreement in Non-Standard French.
Amsterdam, 1981, vii, 113 pp. Paperbound.

II:7. *Jan-Ola Östman*: *You Know*: A Discourse-Functional Study.
Amsterdam, 1981, viii, 91 pp. Paperbound.

II:8. *Claude Zilberberg*: Essai sur les modalités tensives.
Amsterdam, 1981, xi, 154 pp. + 4 folding tables. Paperbound.

III:1. *Ivan Fonagy*: Situation et Signification.
Amsterdam, 1982, v, 160 pp. Paperbound.

III:2/3. *Jürgen Weissenborn and Wolfgang Klein (eds.)*: Here and There. Cross-linguistic Studies in Deixis and Demonstration.
Amsterdam, 1982. v, 296 pp. Paperbound.

III:4. *Waltraud Brennenstuhl*: Control and Ability. Towards a Biocybernetics of Language.
Amsterdam, 1982. v, 123 pp. Paperbound.

III:5.   *Wolfgang Wildgen*: Catastrophe Theoretic Semantics: An Elaboration and Application of René Thom's Theory.
Amsterdam, 1982. iv, 124 pp. Paperbound.

III:6.   *René Dirven, Louis Goossens, Yvan Putseys and Emma Vorlat*: The Scene of Linguistic Action and its Perspectivization by SPEAK, TALK, SAY and TELL.
Amsterdam, 1982. v, 186 pp. Paperbound.

III:7.   *Thomas Ballmer*: Biological Foundations of Linguistic Communication. Towards a Biocybernetics of Language.
Amsterdam, 1982. x, 161 pp. Paperbound.

III:8.   *Douglas N. Walton*: Topical Relevance in Argumentation.
Amsterdam, 1982. viii, 81 pp. Paperbound.

IV:1.   *Marcelo Dascal*: Pragmatics and the Philosophy of Mind. Vol. I.
Amsterdam, 1983. xii, 207 pp. Paperbound.

IV:2.   *Richard Zuber*: Non-declarative Sentences.
Amsterdam, 1983. ix, 123 pp. Paperbound.

IV:3.   *Michel Meyer*: Meaning and Reading. A Philosophical Essay on Language and Literature.
Amsterdam, 1983. ix, 176 pp. Paperbound.

IV:4.   *Walburga von Raffler-Engel*: The Perception of Nonverbal Behavior in the Career Interview.
Amsterdam, 1983. viii, 148 pp. Paperbound.

IV:5.   *Jan Prucha*: Pragmalinguistics: East European Approaches.
Amsterdam, 1983. v, 103 pp. Paperbound.

IV:6.   *Alex Huebler*: Understatements and Hedges in English.
Amsterdam, 1983. ix, 192 pp. Paperbound.

IV:7.   *Herman Parret*: Semiotics and Pragmatics. An Evaluative Comparison of Conceptual Frameworks.
Amsterdam, 1983. xii, 136 pp. Paperbound.

IV:8.   *Jürgen Streeck*: Social Order in Child Communication. A Study in Microethnography.
Amsterdam, 1983. vii, 130 pp. Paperbound.

V:1.   *Marlene Dolitsky*: Under the Tumtum Tree: From Nonsense to Sense, a Study in Non-automatic Comprehension.
Amsterdam, 1984. vii, 119 pp. Paperbound.

V:2.   *Roger G. van de Velde*: Prolegomena to Inferential Discourse Processing.
Amsterdam, 1984. viii, 100 pp. Paperbound.

V:3.   *Teun Van Dijk*: Prejudice in Discourse. An Analysis of Ethnic Prejudice in Cognition and Conversation.
Amsterdam, 1984. x, 170 pp. Paperbound.

V:4.   *Henk Haverkate*: Speech Acts, Speakers and Hearers. Reference and Referential Strategies in Spanish.
Amsterdam, 1984. xi, 142 pp. Paperbound.

V:5.   *Lauri Carlson*: "Well" in Dialogue Games: A Discourse Analysis of the Interjection "Well" in Idealized Conversation.
Amsterdam, 1984 (publ. 1985). ix, 111 pp. Paperbd.

V:6.   *Danilo Marcondes de Souza Filho*: Language and Action: A Reassessment of Speech Act Theory.
Amsterdam, 1984 (publ. 1985). ix, 167 pp. Paperbd.

V:7.	*Lars Qvortrup*: The Social Significance of Telematics: An Essay on the Information Society. Amsterdam, 1984 (publ. 1985). xi, 230 pp. Paperbd.
V:8.	*J.C.P. Auer*: Bilingual Conversation. Amsterdam, 1984 (publ. 1985). ix, 116 pp. Paperbd.
VI:1.	*Jean-Pierre Desclés, Zlatka Guentchéva & Sebastian Shaumyan*: Theoretical Aspects of Passivization in the Framework of Applicative Grammar. Amsterdam, 1985 (publ. 1986). viii, 115 pp. Paperbd.
VI:2.	*Jon-K Adams*: Pragmatics and Fiction. Amsterdam, 1985 (publ. 1986). vi, 77 pp. Paperbd.
VI:3.	*Betsy K. Barnes*: The Pragmatics of Left Detachment in Spoken Standard French. Amsterdam, 1985 (publ. 1986). viii, 123 pp. Paperbd.
VI:4.	*Luigia Camaioni, Cláudia de Lemos, et al.*: Questions on Social Explanation: Piagetian Themes reconsidered. Amsterdam, 1985 (publ. 1986). viii, 141 pp. Paperbd.